NO HIGHER CALLING

Shepherding God's People According to Paul

CRAIG IRELAND

LUCIDBOOKS

No Higher Calling: Shepherding God's People According to Paul

Published by Lucid Books in Houston, TX
www.LucidBooks.com

eISBN: 978-1-63296-553-0
ISBN: 978-1-63296-551-6 (paperback)
ISBN: 978-1-63296-552-3 (hardback)

Special Sales: Most Lucid Books titles are available in special quantity discounts. Custom imprinting or excerpting can also be done to fit special needs. Contact Lucid Books at Info@LucidBooks.com

CONTENTS

Special Thanks go to:

Pastor Aaron Kelley, for his help refining and clarifying some of the phrases and arguments in this book.

Pastor Tom Foord, for his unyielding support and encouragement.

And the many pastors and church leaders who requested this resource be put into print.

Lastly, and most importantly, my wife Katarina, who knows me best and still supports me the most.

Introduction

Why Another Book on Church Leadership?

The shelves of Christian bookstores groan beneath the weight of literature written about leadership. The seemingly endless results of an online search for content addressing church leaders prove that this is not an area lacking attention. My awareness of this became the greatest obstacle in bringing this current work to publication. I am very aware that I do not have anything *new* to say.

However, a curious phenomenon is emerging: while today's church leaders have greater access to resources than ever before, there appears to be more burnout, struggle, moral decline, and resignation than ever before. It is not a lack of leadership material that is causing the ill health of church leaders and their ministries.

The burden of this book is not that it presents something *new* for leaders to try, implement, or utilize. The burden of this book is that everything that is needed for faithful and fruitful ministry has already been well established. Not in the last century, not even in the last millennia, but in the words of Christ's apostles in the New Testament. The Scriptures are entirely sufficient for God's servants to "be complete, equipped for every good work" (2 Timothy 3:17).

What this book represents is a rediscovery of the model and philosophy of ministry that Christ's apostles faithfully handed down to the church. I do believe that in many ways we have strayed from the apostolic and New Testament paradigm of church leadership. If we were able to recapture the ministry philosophy of the Apostle Paul and implement it, then church decline would be radically halted, and church growth would be restored as the norm. Moreover, the church's leaders would be known less for scandals and impropriety, and more as "worker[s] who [have] no need to be ashamed, rightly handling the word of truth" (2 Timothy 2:15).

Leadership Is Everything

Every church rises and falls by its leadership. This is a foundational principle of Scripture that must be understood before any benefit can be derived from a resource like this. In Zechariah 13:7, the Lord prophesied, "Strike the shepherd, and the sheep will be scattered". These words were principally foretelling Jesus and his crucifixion. It prophesied that once Jesus was arrested, his followers would all abandon their delusions of loyalty and scatter (c.f. Matthew 26:31). Behind this astounding prophecy remains the ever-reliable truism that as the leader goes, so goes their followers. If a leader is healthy, reliable, growing, and producing, then their followers, in the main, will follow suit. If a leader is unhealthy, faltering, stunted, and unproductive, then consequently their followers will often imitate this indolence.

Healthy church leaders aspire to be faithful and profitable servants of their Lord (Matthew 25:21, 23). If they are to achieve this, they must rediscover the model and philosophy of ministry found in the example of Christ's inspired apostles. Any leadership theorizing that departs from the leadership demonstrated and taught by Jesus' apostles must be repented of and abandoned.

The challenge of seeking a New Testament paradigm for ministry is that, although the Apostle Paul planted many churches and installed leaders to shepherd these churches, much of his advice and counsel to these leaders has not been preserved (Acts 14:23). While the New Testament is not an exhaustive repository of every morsel of the apostles' leadership instruction, it contains a wealth of inspired pastoral advice. Notably, the epistles to Titus and Timothy contain an abundance of help and guidance. Moreover, in Acts 20:17–38, the Apostle Paul directly addressed the elders of the

Ephesian church, codifying and elucidating what he understood as the essence of gospel ministry. His challenges to these elders are deeply convicting and motivating, revealing what made his ministry so uniquely God-honoring and fruitful.

This book's main purpose will be to bring the ministry philosophy of the Apostle Paul into the 21st century. Supported by the entire Bible, the bulk of this book's content and structure will be derived from Paul's magisterial address recorded in Acts 20.

If you currently serve as a leader in a local Christian church, in any capacity at all, or you have the ambition to do so, then a study of the Apostle Paul's address to the Ephesian elders is vitally important for you.

Background

Ephesus

This Church's Unusual Origins

Ephesus served as the capital of the Roman province of Asia. At the time of the New Testament, it was the Roman Empire's third-largest city with more than 200,000 inhabitants (behind Rome and Alexandria). Among its most esteemed structures was the great temple of Diana/Artemis, Ephesus' cherished goddess. The city was renowned not only for its cult worship and shrines but also for its entertainment. It boasted one of the ancient world's largest amphitheaters reputed to hold somewhere between 25,000 and 50,000 spectators. The Ephesians took great pride in their city, their Olympic-style games, their patron deity, and all things Ephesian.

The gospel's introduction to this vast and proud city was an unusual one. It involved the influence of an enigmatic figure from the early days of Jesus' ministry: John the Baptist. It is only in Ephesus (see Acts 19) that the disciples of John the Baptist are explicitly mentioned after the ascension of Christ. During Paul's first stay[1] at Ephesus, he encountered several of John's disciples who appeared ignorant about the salvific events which transpired after John's beheading, and especially about the outpouring of God's Spirit on the day of Pentecost.

1. This was not Paul's first recorded visit to Ephesus, as Acts 18 records a brief and uneventful excursion through the city in transit back to Syrian Antioch. "And they came to Ephesus, and he left them there, but he himself went into the synagogue and reasoned with the Jews. When they asked him to stay for a longer period, he declined. But on taking leave of them he said, 'I will return to you if God wills,' and he set sail from Ephesus" (Acts 18:19–21).

Luke narrates the sequence of events that lead to the planting of the Ephesian church:

> "While Apollos was in Corinth, Paul traveled through the interior regions and came to Ephesus. He found some disciples and asked them, "Did you receive the Holy Spirit when you believed?"
>
> 'No,' they told him, 'we haven't even heard that there is a Holy Spirit.'
>
> 'Into what then were you baptized?' he asked them.
>
> 'Into John's baptism,' they replied.
>
> Paul said, 'John baptized with a baptism of repentance, telling the people that they should believe in the one who would come after him, that is, in Jesus.'
>
> When they heard this, they were baptized into the name of the Lord Jesus. And when Paul had laid his hands on them, the Holy Spirit came on them, and they began to speak in other tongues and to prophesy. Now there were about twelve men in all. Paul entered the synagogue and spoke boldly for three months, arguing and persuading them about the kingdom of God. But when some became hardened and would not believe, slandering the Way in front of the crowd, he withdrew from them, taking the disciples, and conducted discussions every day in the lecture hall of Tyrannus. This went on for two years, so that all the residents of Asia, both Jews, and Greeks, heard the word of the Lord" (Acts 19:1–10).

It is evident that these disciples belonged to the original group that followed and served John the Baptist. At the time of Paul's arrival in Ephesus, John the Baptist had been dead for approximately two decades. Despite the long passage of time, this small group of twelve members remained firm in their commitment to their leader's doctrine and example. Paul's question, "*Did you receive the Holy Spirit when you believed?*" was a means of verifying whether the good news of Jesus' death, burial and resurrection had been communicated to these disciples. In other words, Paul was utilizing a specific line of inquiry to discern whether these disciples were, in fact, genuine Christians yet. Since they never heard that there even was a Holy Spirit, it was evident to Paul that these disciples were merely prepared in John's baptism for repentance and had not gone any further into the fullness of gospel faith. They remained ignorant of the gift of God's free grace, which is communicated by and through the Holy Spirit, of whom they had not even heard. John the Baptist's disciples readily accepted Paul's testimony, as they had been prepared to do, and submitted to baptism in the name of Jesus. Subsequently, the gift of the Holy Spirit came upon them with accompanying signs to verify their entrance into the New Covenant. In this manner, the church at Ephesus was born.

Paul enjoyed a substantial term of ministry among the Ephesians, and it was probably during this period that he wrote his first epistle to the Corinthians.[2] Paul labored among these new believers around the clock, never hesitating to declare to them the whole counsel of God. The church grew rapidly, and great numbers of new converts were added. Such was the immense fruitfulness of the gospel in Ephesus that the believers were unable to secure a permanent place of worship and began holding their meetings in several homes among the more distinguished members.[3] Soon elders were equipped and appointed to shepherd, exercise pastoral oversight, and continue the miraculous work of building the church.

2. 1 Corinthians was Paul's first *canonical* epistle. 1 Corinthians mentions an earlier letter that has not been preserved in the New Testament.
3. Acts 19:20.

Turmoil, Riot, and Departure

As Ephesians were coming to faith in great numbers, a silversmith named Demetrius sparked a public uproar in response. The smiths made most of their income by fashioning idols and relics for pagan worship. When many Ephesians began to renounce idol worship and turn to Christ, their profits were in grave jeopardy. After a significant loss of business, the smiths began to incite the rest of the people to riot, renouncing Paul, the disciples, and the faith they promoted. This riot spread rapidly, feeding off the anti-Christian sentiment that was also growing in the city. The clerk (a high position commanding great respect and political power) diplomatically quelled the crowds, and Paul prudently took his leave for Macedonia. Even in Paul's absence, the Ephesian church continued to grow and had the privilege of being served by some of the New Testament's most noteworthy ministers, including Apollos, John the Beloved, and Timothy.

After some time, Paul determined to make another visit to Jerusalem even after being warned that great hardship and persecution awaited him there. Paul, feeling compelled to arrive at Jerusalem in time for the festival of Pentecost, chose not to detour to Ephesus again. However, sensing this might be his last opportunity to address and encourage the elders, he called them to join him at the port of Miletus to receive their final instructions (Acts 20:16–18).

Paul's Magisterial Address

The context above sets the stage for Paul's magisterial address (Acts 20:18–38),

> You yourselves know how I lived among you the whole time from the first day that I set foot in Asia, serving the Lord with all humility and with tears and with trials that happened to me through the plots of the Jews; how I did not shrink from declaring to you anything that was profitable and teaching you in public and from

house to house, testifying both to Jews and Greeks of repentance toward God and faith in our Lord Jesus Christ. And now, behold, I am going to Jerusalem, constrained by the Spirit, not knowing what will happen to me there, except that the Holy Spirit testifies to me in every city that imprisonment and afflictions await me. But I do not account my life of any value nor as precious to myself, if only I may finish my course and the ministry that I received from the Lord Jesus, to testify to the gospel of the grace of God. And now, behold, I know that none of you among whom I have gone about proclaiming the kingdom will see my face again. Therefore, I testify to you this day that I am innocent of the blood of all, for I did not shrink from declaring to you the whole counsel of God. Pay careful attention to yourselves and to all the flock, in which the Holy Spirit has made you overseers, to care for the church of God, which he obtained with his own blood. I know that after my departure fierce wolves will come in among you, not sparing the flock; and from among your own selves will arise men speaking twisted things, to draw away the disciples after them. Therefore, be alert, remembering that for three years I did not cease night or day to admonish every one with tears. And now I commend you to God and to the word of his grace, which is able to build you up and to give you the inheritance among all those who are sanctified. I coveted no one's silver or gold or apparel. You yourselves know that these hands ministered to my necessities and to those who were with me. In all things I have shown you that by working hard in this way we must help the weak and remember the words of the Lord Jesus, how he himself said, 'It is more blessed to give than to receive.'

And when he had said these things, he knelt down and prayed with them all. And there was much weeping on the part of all; they embraced Paul and kissed him, being sorrowful most of all because of the word he had spoken, that they would not see his face again. And they accompanied him to the ship.

Final Words

"And now I know that none of you, among whom I went about preaching the kingdom, will ever see me again" (vs. 25).

To get a sense of the force of the Apostle Paul's speech to these elders, we must consider it as though it conveyed his final words (something akin to a deathbed confession). At the time of delivering this address, Paul himself was convinced that this was the last time he would have the opportunity to meet with these elders. This explains his state of mind and the conviction with which he issued this stirring charge. As we trace the history of Paul's relationship with this church, we learn that this will not be Paul's last occasion to address the Ephesians. Luke will go on to narrate the apostle's arrival in Rome, where he was put under house arrest, and from where he wrote his Epistle to the Ephesians. Paul would later issue two more epistles for the benefit of the Ephesian church in writing to their pastor, Timothy. Nevertheless, what must remain in focus when analyzing this speech in Acts 20 is that Paul spoke under the weight of the conviction that these would be his final words to these men.

The Multiplicity of Words

In an average lifetime, it is estimated that a person will speak somewhere between 123 million and an astonishing 860 million words.

Some words are immensely important, such as wedding vows pledged at the marriage altar. Most of the millions of words spoken are far less significant. For example, most of us would not like to have our words recorded while we endure the spectacle of our favorite sporting team losing against their rival.

Some of the words we utter we would do almost anything to retract, such as a hurtful remark to our spouse in the heat of an argument, or a discouraging line to one of our children when they have exhausted our finite patience. Sometimes words are just spoken to fill an awkward silence. Not every word spoken carries the same degree of importance or consequence.

The Significance of Words

Jesus offered his insight as to the significance of words when he declared that every careless word spoken will be weighed in the balance of God's judgment.

> "The good person out of his good treasure brings forth good, and the evil person out of his evil treasure brings forth evil. I tell you, on the day of judgment people will give account for every careless word they speak, for by your words you will be justified, and by your words you will be condemned" (Matthew 12:35–37).

James rightly warned, "For we all stumble in many ways. And if anyone does not stumble in what he says, he is a perfect man, able also to bridle his whole body" (James 3:2).

The tongue is incredibly powerful in that it reveals what thoughts and feelings are concealed inside of a person. Jesus taught that, ". . . out of the abundance of the heart the mouth speaks" (Matthew 12:34). In one sense then, every utterance is also insight into something true about the speaker. If someone is disposed to speak trivially on all occasions, without regard for their words, then the words themselves may not be a revelation of the content of their heart, but they will be a revelation of the condition of their heart.

It is a fearful thought to consider that every word we have ever uttered will be called into account on the great day of God's judgment. Since words reveal the true content and condition of our hearts, when God takes our words and casts them in the light of his judgment, he is thereby also judging the thoughts and intentions of our hearts.

If you are a Christian, then take a moment to sigh with relief as one who is redeemed by grace through faith, all on account of another's righteousness—the impeccably holy Jesus Christ. But don't sigh quite so hard that you forget just how valuable words can be. We are told that God created the universe and sustains every atom of its makeup by the Word of his power (Hebrews 1:3). Though our words are not divine and do not carry God's omnipotence, our words have weight. Reflecting on the power and severity of words, as well as our frivolous use of them, is time very well spent.

The Commodity of Words

Words can take on greater value as the time and opportunity to voice them ebbs away. When time is short, there is an inherent economy in the employment of words.

Would you plan to speak to others differently if you suddenly realized that you had only one week to live? If you were down to a single day left in this world, would you communicate with different words and phrases than what you might otherwise? We would all exercise far greater care if we learned that the next few words we uttered would be our last. Perhaps, like the Apostle Paul, we would exercise maximal caution if we were down to our last moments and were addressing a group of people into whom we had invested our life, and upon whose success all our labor rests.

By putting ourselves in this frame of mind, we begin to enter Paul's predicament as we approach an exploration of his address in Acts 20.

No one wastes their breath with trivialities when delivering their final words. That's not to say people can't be light-hearted or offer some humorous remarks in their final moments, as is often the case when a family is surrounding the bed of a dear departing one. But everything that is said is assessed by its necessity. In someone's final words, they summarize everything needful and give force and weight precisely where they believe it ought to be.

Among all of Paul's speeches in the New Testament, this one deserves special treatment and emphasis. As far as he knew, this was his last admonition to a group of men that he had spilled his own blood, sweat, and tears in serving, mentoring, and deploying. Now, after giving them his very life in labor and devotion, he is offering them this final service. In this speech, he charges them and prays with them, commending them to God and the Word of his grace. This gracious Word, Paul promised, "is able to build them up and to give them an inheritance among all those who are sanctified" (Acts 20:32).

Because Paul issued this charge to church leaders as his final instructions, it's my conviction that this speech is the prism through which church leaders of every age must understand their ministry. Only by sufficiently appreciating the necessity of this speech, and comprehending the instruction thereof, can we ever hope to be fit shepherds of Christ's sheep.

No Ordinary Apostle

Matthew Henry is one of the most respected and consulted Bible commentators throughout all of church history. He was a man entirely devoted to God, respected as both a master expositor and faithful pastor. George Whitefield recounts a scene from the end of Henry's life, saying:

> "Matthew Henry, when he was about to expire, said to a friend, 'You have heard many men's dying words, and these are mine: A

> life spent in communion with God, is the pleasantest life in the world.'"[4]

The above quote is very endearing, often shared, and considered authoritative in commending a life dedicated to communion with God. It is predominantly due to the high esteem Matthew Henry is afforded that his final words carry such weight and force.

When we approach Paul's address to the Ephesian elders, which he believed to be his last, we ought to approach it with deep solemnity and the conviction that these words are of ultimate importance.

Speaking about himself, Paul attested,

> "According to the grace of God given to me, like a skilled master builder I laid a foundation, and someone else is building upon it. Let each one take care how he builds upon it" (1 Corinthians 3:10).

Paul was no ordinary apostle. He exercised great skill as a master builder laying a foundation for the entire future church of God. Undoubtedly, this assessment speaks broadly of all of Paul's kingdom labor. And yet, this foundation must refer principally to the canonization of Paul's epistles. Paul's inspired writings became the bedrock for the New Testament and for any church that desires to be in continuity with the apostles. When we encounter Paul's speech in Acts 20:17–35, we are reading words weighed and uttered by the apostolic master-builder of Christ's church. This apostle is someone that all elders and pastors should aspire to emulate as they fulfill their role as servant-builders constructing on his foundation.[5]

4. Whitefield, George. *The Sermons of George Whitefield. Vol. 1.* Wheaton, IL: Crossway, 2012. pg. 76

5. "Be imitators of me, as I am of Christ" (1 Corinthians 11:1).

How Should We Approach?

We must approach this speech with humility, listening as though we were one of those very elders representing the Ephesian church. We must stand with them and hear Paul's words as our highest charge to serve in the Household of God, with honor, zeal, discipline, and apostolic purpose. We ought to accept every instruction as coming directly from Paul to us, and every warning should cause us deep concern. We should approach with a high sense of gratitude for the Lord's graciousness in allowing us to come near to witness such a solemn scene. Lastly, we should pray that the Lord enables us to partake in this speech's treasure as we seek to serve in a manner worthy of our high calling.

The Holy Spirit Makes Overseers

> *"Pay careful attention to yourselves and to all the flock, in which* ***the Holy Spirit has made you overseers****, to care for the church of God, which he obtained with his own blood"* (Acts 20:28, emphasis added).

Here is the crux of Paul's entire speech. We will deal with the injunctions and implications of this verse in Chapter 6, but for now, our focus will be retained on these simple yet powerful words: "the Holy Spirit has made you overseers."

Every person serving the church in a leadership role (pastors, bishops, elders, leaders, etc.) is the target of both Paul's speech and this very book. Those who do not yet hold formal church office, but aspire to do so, must also pay very close attention to how the apostle addressed these Ephesian elders.

Before we continue our discussion, we should understand that the titles "overseer", "elder", "pastor", and "bishop" overlap in the Scripture to such a degree that many consider these terms to be interchangeable and synonymous. Exploring the elaborate debate on the use of these titles and investigating their continuity or discontinuity is beyond the scope of this book. What is important is that in Paul's address, these elders functioned as the overseers (bishops) and pastors (shepherds) of the church at Ephesus. For the purpose of this book, the assumption will be made that these titles are interchangeable and represent the many different functions and duties of church leaders. These particular men who were summoned by Paul from Ephesus to meet him in Miletus are called "elders" (Gk. *Presbuteros* in vs. 17). They are told that it was the Holy Spirit who has made them "overseers" (Gk. *Epískopos,* which is the root word for our modern English word "bishop," in vs. 28). Finally, they are commanded to "feed" the church (vs. 28). The word "feed" is translated from the Greek word "*poimainó,*" meaning to shepherd or pastor. This level of interchangeability may not be mirrored in every instance where these words appear in the New Testament; but on this occasion, Paul has no problem utilizing them to refer to the same group of men who functioned as the Ephesian church's highest level of leadership.

What Paul stresses unambiguously is that it is "the Holy Spirit [who] has made . . . [them] overseers,". This statement includes three implications:

1. It is the Holy Spirit's unique work to make overseers.
2. The making of an overseer is entirely by grace.
3. God makes overseers for his own glory.

1. It is the Holy Spirit's Unique Work to Make Overseers

In answering the question of who it is that makes overseers, the text is clear: it is the particular work of the Holy Spirit.

The Holy Spirit is truly God. God is one Being existing eternally in three distinct Persons. This is a formulation that is both uncontrovertibly scriptural and cheerfully embraced by the Christian church since the age of the apostles. This formulation has come to be understood as the doctrine of the Holy Trinity. At the root of this doctrine is the scriptural revelation that the Lord God is one undivided essence. The Old and New Testaments further demonstrate that this indivisible essence is exhausted in three distinct Persons, the Father, the Son, and the Holy Spirit.[6]

6. "Exhausted" is the right verb here because the three Persons of the Trinity do not share in the essence as to occupy a portion of the whole (this would mean that the essence is divisible, and each Person is only partly divine). Each Person is truly and exhaustively God in every sense of the word, and as such, they each possess the divine essence in total. However, each Person remains distinct and distinguishable from each other, relating to each other and working out their plan together in creation and redemption.

Each of these Persons is truly God, perfectly relating to each other from all eternity, and occupying unique roles in both creation and redemption. In the economy of redemption, the objective work of salvation is ascribed to the meritorious life, death, and resurrection of Jesus Christ the Son. The application of this salvation is the unique responsibility of the Holy Spirit. This also includes the protection, the equipping, and the empowerment of the ordinary ministry of Christ's church. Paul appropriately stresses that it is the Holy Spirit who specifically performs the work of making, gifting, equipping, and mobilizing overseers to shepherd the flock of God.

In the experience of local church elders, knowing that they have been called and commissioned by the Holy Spirit is no small matter. Generally speaking, it can make a striking difference to the enjoyment of executing a task when a person considers *who* it is that calls and directs them to undertake it.

Take a moment and imagine a task that was truly noble and very desirable. What would it be like if you were called upon to be the favored person to take up such a task? What a delight that would be! Now, imagine that the person who appointed and directed you to do such a thing was someone you passionately despised. Rather than this great privilege bringing you full delight, the joy is now mingled with distaste, and the entire task might soon become burdensome, if not loathsome.

For example, consider the role of a saboteur who during wartime is sent undercover into enemy territory to gather intel. Although he may rise high through the leadership ranks of his enemies, it wouldn't matter how much social and political altitude he gained or how sought-after his position was; he could never truly savor the privilege, though outwardly he must continue the charade. While he is undercover, he makes a full showing of support for the regime he despises and seeks to undermine. He follows his superiors' orders, feigning compliance, and yet continually seeks opportunities to undermine and destabilize his enemy. Ultimately, he answers to those who sent him on this clandestine mission, but more immediately, he must obey and submit to the authority of his enemy, hoping to secure their trust. Every single task he is ordered to perform by the enemy is innately abhorrent, not because the tasks themselves are awful, but because he is being ordered to perform them by someone endeavoring to destroy what he loves: his homeland, his family, and his freedoms.

Conversely, if we are directed to engage in a task that's innately menial, detestable, even onerous, and we have been appointed to such a duty by someone that we love deeply and esteem highly, performing that task brings with it a unique relish.

For example, consider a young couple who are just experiencing the earliest flourishing of their affection. Lovers in this state will often endure the most debasing acts if it demonstrates their true feelings for the object of their love. They will gladly humble themselves and go to the most extreme efforts to prove their love even when such behavior and devotion are entirely unfathomable in any other context. Most of us have born witness to how youthful love can often debase those captivated by it. Have you ever had the misfortune of witnessing a youthful couple speaking to each other in babyish voices or inappropriately canoodling in a public place? Although outsiders find their expressions of affection exaggerated and even odious, those experiencing this infatuation show no signs of knowing or caring what others think.

The Apostle Paul makes it clear that those who serve the church as her ministers have been made overseers by the highest authority, the greatest good, and the purest love. Overseers must consider their charge as the most honorable in all creation. This is not necessarily because of the functions of their calling (at times church leaders are tasked with the most ignoble work), but because of *who* has called them and positioned them to serve.

We see this principle demonstrated in the example of heavenly angels. John Newton, the famed author of the hymn, "Amazing Grace," once reflected on the experience of angels in serving the Lord. Angels are both mysterious and fascinating beings, but this much is sure: they locate their joy in the privilege of serving and obeying the Person whom they love supremely, regardless of the task he commissions for them.

He wrote,

> "If two angels were to receive at the same moment a commission from God, one to go down and rule earth's grandest empire, the other to go and sweep the streets of its meanest village, it would be a matter of entire indifference to each which service fell to his lot, the post of ruler or the post of scavenger; for the joy of the angels lies only in obedience to God's will, and with equal joy, they would lift a Lazarus in his rags to Abraham's bosom, or be a chariot of fire to carry an Elijah home."[7]

Church overseers and leaders must actively and regularly remind themselves of the One that has elevated them. In doing this they are not only afforded an opportunity to locate their joy in the privilege of serving so great a Lord, but they are also freed from a multitude of frustrations and temptations that would otherwise devour them and contaminate their ministry.

When overseers have this truth pressed upon them by way of reminder, it enables them to enjoy the freedom of putting others' opinions in perspective, regardless of whether they are positive or negative.

7. Bounds, Edward M. *The Essentials of Prayer*. Dallas, TX: Gideon House Books, 2016. Print.

The great power in remembering *who* has called the church's elders and overseers is that it frees them from the man-pleasing that renders so many good ministers compromised and, in turn, obsolete. To the Galatians, Paul wrote, "For am I now seeking the approval of man, or of God? Or am I trying to please man? If I were still trying to please man, I would not be a servant of Christ" (Galatians 1:10). These two objectives are at odds with each other. One cannot be seeking the approval of man while at the same time trying to serve God, just as one can never serve two opposing masters (Matthew 6:24).

Many ministers commence their service in the church well. They run with zeal and hold fast the word of truth. However, the constant pressure of the office, the incessant complaints of naysayers, and the praise of the politically motivated will all eventually turn the minister's attention away from God who called him, to chase the whims of a fickle crowd. This is the death knell for any ministry, regardless of how powerful and fruitful it may have once been. As soon as the voices of the people surrounding a minister become louder and more influential than the voice of the Holy Spirit in the Scriptures, that ministry is dead even while it appears to live (1 Timothy 5:6, Revelation 3:1).

Ministers must always, regardless of how pervasive and powerful every other influence is, remember *who* has made them and seek to please him exclusively. Just as "no soldier gets entangled in civilian pursuits, since his aim is to please the one who enlisted him," so it is with overseers who are called and appointed by the Holy Spirit (2 Timothy 2:4). Ministers must commit to being single-minded and reflect often upon the necessity to seek to please the One who enlists them, to the exclusion of all others.

The point is not that ministers can be entirely ignorant of the opinions of others and forge ahead disregarding what feedback others offer. It does, however, grant leaders the ability to keep others' opinions in proper perspective. The opinions of others may do well as servants, but only God's Word has the right to be master over our thoughts, feelings, and actions.

Once overseers have achieved this balance, they will find it incredibly mind-clearing and liberating. There are times in a minister's life when the outward clamoring of voices pull in a thousand different directions. When one can block out that noise and recall that they have been commissioned to serve and please one Master, then every other distraction loses its sway. As the minister dials in his mental focus, keeping it centered on the Lord and his calling, he inevitably experiences the beauty and calmness that comes to those who wait on the Lord, for they "shall renew their strength; they shall mount up with wings like eagles; they shall run and not be weary; they shall walk and not faint" (Isaiah 40:31).

Minsters intuitively know that it is impossible to please everyone. As ministers grow in experience, there's one reality that becomes painfully clear: the quickest and most effective way to offend the maximal number of people is to try and please them all. Knowing this as objective truth, however, doesn't seem to liberate overseers from falling into the rut of expending energy trying to keep people happy. The only preventative against this trap is the intentional reminder that "You are not your own, for you were bought with a price. So glorify God in your body" (1 Corinthians 6:19b).

Moreover, because it is the Holy Spirit who has established the church's "overseers," they have the freedom and empowerment to endure any trial, whether internal or external.

Those who have experience serving as overseers already know that the attacks and ambushes endured by ministers are varied, constant, often unpredictable, and deeply wearying. Jesus warned every believer that trials will come (John 16:33). The privileged assurance that every Christian enjoys is not that the Lord has prescribed an easy life, but that "The steps of a man are established by the LORD, when he delights in his way" (Psalm 37:23).

When trials come, a minister can derive much-needed encouragement and strength from remembering *who* has called him to suffer and endure them. Just as the elder's calling into the ministry does not come from within himself, so it is with the fortitude needed to endure trials. Every trial is authored by the sovereign decree of an infinite, loving, all-wise, and almighty God. Every minister's confidence is that the One who calls them into service as overseers will undoubtedly sustain them amid any trial. Yet God's promise is greater still: not only will the Lord sustain his servants, but he will also transform their trial into a dutiful servant which will refine them as gold—purified by fire (1 Peter 1:6–7).

Any minister laboring under the delusion that their calling as an overseer emerged from within themselves will never endure the extraordinary trials that ministry brings. By remembering that it is the Holy Spirit who calls and directs leaders into the ministry, they are assured, even in their darkest hour, that he will sustain them and cause all things to "work together for good" (Romans 8:28).

One of the most dramatic examples of this was the experience of Adoniram and Ann Judson who served as missionaries in Burma (modern-day Myanmar) in the first half of the 19th century. Ann Judson reflects on her experience of suffering the inexpressible pain of losing the lives of their two children, one at sea during the voyage out to the mission field, and the second who was born and survived only a few short years with them in the field. Soon a third child was born to the missionary couple, but their joy was short-lived. War was declared between England and Burma and Adoniram was arrested and confined in the death camp where none were expected to survive. Ann grew emotionally and physically weary after several heroic, yet unsuccessful, attempts to obtain her husband's release. While she remained responsible for the mission base that they built and continued tending to both her husband's daily needs and her newborn daughter, she fell deathly ill. She speaks about how acute her sufferings were and how desperate her situation had become. If it were not for the eternal reality of God's sovereignty and benevolence, she could not have born her "accumulated sufferings."

She wrote,

> "When in health, I could bear the various trials and vicissitudes through which I was called to pass. But to be confined with sickness, and unable to assist those who were so dear to me, when in distress, was almost too much for me to bear; and had it not been for the consolations of religion, and an assured conviction that every additional trial was ordered by infinite love and mercy, I must have sunk under my accumulated sufferings."[8]

Just as it is true for every believer, ministers have a guarantee that trials will come. However, ministers should expect that their trials will be more severe, more frequent, and more specifically engineered to bring about their public failure. When trials come, overseers must actively remind themselves that the strength to prevail is never found within themselves. This strength can only come from the Holy Spirit, and "if the Spirit of him who raised Jesus from the dead dwells in you, he who raised Christ Jesus from the dead will also give life to your mortal bodies through his Spirit who dwells in you" (Romans 8:11).

Lastly, because it is the Holy Spirit who has made the church's overseers, they have the freedom and power to resist all temptations.

8. Wayland, F. *A Memoir of the Life and Labors of the Rev. Adoniram Judson*. D.D. United Kingdom: Phillips, Sampson, 1853. pg. 347.

Much like trials, temptations are an ever-present reality in the lives of all believers. God has appointed specific means of grace that Christians must employ in their battle against temptations to sin: prayer, Scripture, the ordinances of Baptism and the Lord's Supper, and fellowship with other believers. These means are not efficacious in themselves, but the Spirit uses them to convey sin-killing power and grace for growth in sanctification and Christlikeness.

While most overseers are already aware of this, they must know that they have a much greater need for reliance on the Holy Spirit than the average believer does. The Holy Spirit takes a very personal interest in every minister's sanctification. Therefore, when temptation comes, as it certainly will, it is on the Spirit that leaders must depend.

It should be obvious to all that the tempter employs greater and more potent weaponry against those who are commissioned as guardians and ministers of Christ's flock. Overseers should never think that they will be left to the ordinary assaults of the enemy when a victory over them often occasions great victory over the ones that they shepherd. Scripture itself says, "Strike the shepherd, and the sheep will be scattered" (Zechariah 13:7).

Richard Baxter vividly describes the true source of Satan's malice against Christ's overseers:

> "Take heed to yourselves, because the tempter will more ply you with his temptations than other men. If you will be the leaders against the prince of darkness, he will spare you no further than God restrained him. He bears the greatest malice to those that are engaged to do him the greatest mischief. As he hates Christ more than any of us, because he is the General of the field, the Captain of our salvation, and does more than all the world besides against his kingdom; so does he hate the leaders under [Christ], more than the common soldiers: he knows what a [crushing defeat]

> he may make among them, if the leaders fall before their eyes (Hebrews 2:10)."[9]

For overseers to harbor even a scintilla of confidence that they are robust enough to resist the enemy is the manifestation of unfettered pride. Worse still, it shows that the enemy has already gained ascendancy over them as his prey. Every minister must know that only an abiding childlike dependence on the Holy Spirit can empower them to face the flood of temptation that they will be forced to resist.

While the devil feverishly seeks the ruin of all Christ's ministers, the Holy Spirit actively works for their relief and strengthening. Paul affirms this process, saying,

> "Therefore, let anyone who thinks that he stands take heed lest he fall. No temptation has overtaken you that is not common to man. God is faithful, and he will not let you be tempted beyond your ability, but with the temptation he will also provide the way of escape, that you may be able to endure it" (1 Corinthians 10:12–13).

Just as the Scriptures promise that "he will also provide the way of escape," that way of escape will never be through dependence on self. Those who look within themselves for the necessary power to endure temptation are prone to collapse under the weakest pressure.

The means of grace available to the overseer do not differ from that which is available to every Christian. The difference is that a wise overseer makes more-than-regular use of these means to get all the grace he can to withstand in the hour of temptation.

9. Baxter, R. *The Reformed Pastor, Showing the Nature of the Pastoral Work*. United Kingdom: T.Ward & Company, 1656. pg. 32.

A wise overseer does not settle for the rudimentary prayer life of most believers because he understands he has far greater needs. The same is true with his meditation and consumption of Scripture. The wise overseer does not assume that what is suitable for the average Christian is also suitable for him. Rather, he seeks to ingest far more Scripture, knowing that the temptations he will be forced to endure are far more potent. The puritan Thomas Watson wrote of the glory and the happiness that the Lord enjoys when his people attend to the means of grace. He paraphrased the Lord's command to his children like this,

> "Go to the ordinances, get as much grace as you can, dig out as much salvation as you can; and the more happiness you have, the more I shall count myself glorified!"[10]

Ministers, if you're going to stand firm in the hour of temptation, do not rest satisfied in only achieving the standard ration of God's goodness through the means of grace. Seek to be a diligent and zealous minor who doesn't rest until he has unearthed all the gold he can from the deep mines of God's grace.

To the broader Ephesian church, the Apostle Paul counseled,

> "Finally, be strong in the Lord and in the strength of his might. Put on the whole armor of God, that you may be able to stand against the schemes of the devil. For we do not wrestle against flesh and blood, but against the rulers, against the authorities, against the cosmic powers over this present darkness, against the spiritual forces of evil in the heavenly places. Therefore take up the whole armor of God, that you may be able to withstand in the evil day, and having done all, to stand firm" (Ephesians 6:10–13).

10. A Body of Practical Divinity in a Series of Sermons on the Shorter Catechism. (n.d.). (n.p.): Lulu.com. Pg. 24.

2. The Making of an Overseer Is Entirely by Grace

If it is the Holy Spirit who makes overseers, then those who are called to the office never have to bear the crippling burden and corrosive effects of pride and self-promotion.

Simply put, because elders do not make themselves overseers, whatever good and giftedness are in them is not of their own doing. Their graces are no credit to them whatsoever.

Ministers who strut, exhibiting themselves with pomp and boasting, fail in their duty and calling in two distinct ways.

First, because Scripture forbids all such boasting. Paul sets the example for us: "But far be it from me to boast except in the cross of our Lord Jesus Christ, by which the world has been crucified to me, and I to the world" (Galatians 6:14).

What foolishness it is to boast in a gift that you have freely received! What credit is it to overseers that they've been given God's grace to lead? Overseers didn't earn it. It was freely bestowed on account of our Lord Jesus Christ—who became sin for us, so that in him we might become the righteousness of God (1 Corinthians 5:21).

Paul wrote to the Galatians that the only ground for boasting in the Christian life is in the cross. By it, all worldly systems, deceptions, pomp, parading, and pride are dead, and church leaders must remain crucified to them all.

Second, because boasting about someone else's work robs them of the glory and honor that they're due. In this instance, such boasting robs the Holy Spirit of the glory that he alone deserves.

Whenever overseers are tempted to take credit for any success in ministry, whether a fruitful season, a growing ministry, or some triumph of the gospel through their ministration, they must remember that they did not make themselves overseers. Therefore, every success that an overseer enjoys must tend to God's glory alone.

If God has granted a gift, a talent, a ministry, or a calling, then let the recipient take special care to never allow that gift to cultivate in them the cancer of pride. Overseers must combat pride with all the power the Spirit of God grants. Every ounce of tribute and appreciation they receive on account of their calling must be returned to God as praise and gratitude. God's ministers are only ever conduits of the acclaim that rightly belongs to him.

Consequently, because elders do not make themselves overseers, whatever goodness or giftedness they possess remains God's work and as such, they are always sufficient to perform his will.

Hudson Taylor, the renowned missionary of the 19th century, put it most succinctly when he stated, "Depend upon it, God's work, done in God's way, will never lack God's supplies."[11]

Overseers are often plagued and hindered by insecurity. They may find themselves reflecting upon other ministries that appear bigger, more successful, better resourced, or more sought-after than their own and feel discouraged. This is one of the most common struggles that ministers endure and, at the same time, one of the least addressed. Even though the Scriptures forbid such comparisons, it is frustratingly difficult for ministers to resist the temptation to measure themselves against other leaders, churches, ministries, etc. Paul exposes this tendency among the ministers in his own day:

11.Taylor, H. *The Story of the China Inland Mission*. United Kingdom: Morgan & Scott, 1900. pg. 238.

> "Not that we dare to classify or compare ourselves with some of those who are commending themselves. But when they measure themselves by one another and compare themselves with one another, they are without understanding" (2 Corinthians 10:12).

Rather, ministers are God's workmanship. While that means that they are still a work in progress, ever stirring up and enhancing their gifts, they should take courage that the Holy Spirit who made them what they are will sufficiently equip them to do his will (2 Timothy 1:6).

If overseers have been diligent to stir up their gifts and develop their ministerial talents, then they must rest in the sovereignty of God over their lives and ministry. Perhaps church leaders might suppose that if they were sovereign over themselves, they would do things differently. Maybe they would give themselves different gifts and abilities, or grant more influence, success, or a greater platform. But this is mere presumption. Overseers will do well to remember that their lot is cast by infinite wisdom and eternal love. Let them strive for greater fruitfulness and even greater faithfulness—fully convinced that they have not made themselves but are the working product of the Holy Spirit.

What overseers need is less attention on themselves and more focus on the One who has made them overseers. Through meditating on this truth, ministers are liberated from that self-obsession that hamstrings so many ministers and ministries today.

3. God Makes Overseers for His Own Glory

Does it not seem strange that the Holy Spirit, in securing the prosperity and success of the gospel, ordains churches to be led by *human* overseers?

I wonder if we, left to ourselves, would have come up with such a plan. From a human standpoint, it seems exceedingly high-risk, dangerous, and fraught with difficulty. There's something very disconcerting about the appointment of weak, sin-prone humans to shepherd God's flock. Yet this is precisely the sovereign plan of God. If you're reading this and you're not yet an overseer, maybe this seems a little drastic and even uncalled for. But for many who are already in the ministry, we might look at ourselves and think, "Really, Lord? Me!? Was this the plan?"

God's appointment of human under-shepherds should strike us with amazement. We should be humbled and even a little terrified by the fact that the sovereign Lord has founded his church at the purchase of the blood of Christ and then decreed that this church would be led by imperfect, finite, sinful men.

It would be beyond intimidating if Tiger Woods approached you one day and requested you to take his son out and teach him how to swing a golf club. How would you feel if Michael Phelps called on you to take one of his children and teach them how to swim? It is highly likely you would very respectfully but firmly decline. It would simply be too much pressure, principally because you know that their respective fathers would do a far better job at teaching those skills than yourself (even if you considered yourself to be quite proficient at golf or swimming).

Yet, how much more intimidating, and even mystifying, is it when the Holy Spirit calls upon feeble men to train up his children in holiness? What an astonishing marvel it is when the Great Shepherd calls upon frail men to shepherd his flock as their ministers!

Never think lightly of the call to ministry. Be sure to reflect often upon the fact that, as ministers, we have not appointed or commissioned ourselves. Therefore, overseers must never indulge in vain self-promotion or self-congratulating. Overseers must remember that the Holy Spirit has called them, not because they are the best, most noble, most holy, or even the most qualified, but because he aims to obtain all the praise, honor, and glory due to his name. As Paul himself says,

> "For the foolishness of God is wiser than men, and the weakness of God is stronger than men. For consider your calling, brothers: not many of you were wise according to worldly standards, not many were powerful, not many were of noble birth. But God chose what is foolish in the world to shame the wise; God chose what is weak in the world to shame the strong; God chose what is low and despised in the world, even things that are not, to bring to nothing things that are, so that no human being might boast in the presence of God. And because of him you are in Christ Jesus, who became to us wisdom from God, righteousness and sanctification and redemption, so that, as it is written, 'Let the one who boasts, boast in the Lord'" (1 Corinthians 1:25–31).

The Church Matters

"Now from Miletus, he sent to Ephesus and summoned the elders of the church" (Acts 20:17).

The Church of Jesus Christ Is Never Peripheral to the Cause of God in the World

When Jesus had finished his mission on earth and was preparing to return to his Father in heaven, he told his disciples, "And behold, I am sending the promise of my Father upon you. But stay in the city until you are clothed with power from on high" (Luke 24:49). He issued both a promise to send "the promise" and a command to "stay . . . until you are clothed in power." He also gave them this assurance: "you will receive power when the Holy Spirit has come upon you, and you will be my witnesses in Jerusalem and in all Judea and Samaria, and to the end of the earth" (Acts 1:8).

The story of the Book of Acts records the triumph of the Spirit of God in the spread of the gospel from Jerusalem, throughout Judea, into the regions of Samaria, and to the ends of the known world. The story comes to a jarring halt with the Apostle Paul in Rome testifying to the gospel of the grace of God unhindered and with all boldness (Acts 28:31). The book represents a thrilling account of God using weak and imperfect servants through their suffering and sacrifice, to establish gospel-preaching churches in all the major centers of the Roman Empire. All of this was to fulfill the promise that the Lord's kingdom will make its inevitable and unstoppable advance upon the kingdom of darkness throughout this world.

It is significant to note that, wherever the gospel took root, a community of faith emerged. Our New Testament bears witness that the Lord cherishes and protects his church whenever it is duly established on gospel truth and dependent on the Spirit's power.

Some years before there was anything akin to a New Testament church, Jesus prophesied, ". . . I will build my church and the gates of hell shall not prevail against it" (Matthew 16:18b). In Jesus' estimation, the churches of the New Testament were never peripheral to the cause of the gospel and the salvation of multitudes of sinners. The church was always Jesus' plan from the very beginning. As such, when we read the narrative of the book of Acts and the rest of the New Testament, Jesus' apostles are not only laboring to win souls, but they are also striving to establish gospel-preaching, disciple-making, and self-multiplying communities. Ministries today face the temptation to see the church as merely one among many worthy projects. With the prevalence of parachurch ministries, nonprofit organizations, and other Christian institutions, churches often invest significant resources into endeavors that do not principally win souls or build the local church. To be sure, many of these organizations do great work, but they are not the primary means Christ has ordained for gospel success. The church is his method for harvesting the precious souls of the lost. Overseers should treasure the centrality of their church in the cause of the gospel. They should seek to focus the lion's share of their energy and resources to strengthen Christ's means for the triumph of the gospel—the local church.

Both Heaven and Hell Will Be Directly Affected

Jesus' prophecy that he ". . . will build [his] church and the gates of hell shall not prevail against it" must fortify the churches' overseers and endue them with confidence that the Lord loves his church and seeks its prosperity and success. In fact, both heaven and hell will be eternally affected by the triumph of the gospel through the church of Jesus Christ.

> "The mission of all missions is the church, and the mission of the church is missions" (Anon).

Heaven will be affected because the mission of the church is the Great Commission. The church's principal aim is to communicate the precious news of God's grace to sinners bringing them into kingdom citizenship and adoption into the family of God. Subsequently, the mission of the church is to encourage, embolden, mobilize, and mature believers for greater fruitfulness in anticipation of the Day of Christ's return.

Paul wrote in Ephesians 2:19, "So then you are no longer strangers and aliens, but you are fellow citizens with the saints and members of the household of God." Here we observe that the New Testament has no category for Christians without meaningful affiliation to a church or "God's Household." If we are in God's family, then we must be actively connected to his Household.

Rather than simply offering an added benefit to our Christian walk, the church is central to what Jesus is doing in us and throughout the world. Through his church, Jesus is calling people from every tribe, nation, and tongue to be his special possession and enjoy eternal fellowship with him in glory. Therefore, heaven will be directly affected by the success and prosperity of the local church.

Thankfully, Jesus has made ample provision for the church's success. Paul explains,

> "And he [Jesus] gave the apostles, the prophets, the evangelists, the shepherds and teachers, to equip the saints for the work of ministry, for building up the body of Christ, until we all attain to the unity of the faith and of the knowledge of the Son of God, to mature manhood, to the measure of the stature of the fullness of Christ, so that we may no longer be children, tossed to and fro by the waves and carried about by every wind of doctrine, by human

> cunning, by craftiness in deceitful schemes. Rather, speaking the truth in love, we are to grow up in every way into him who is the head, into Christ . . ." (Ephesians 4:11–15).

The Lord has given his church the various offices of apostles, prophets, evangelists, shepherds, and teachers to equip the saints and build up the body. Every believer is called to commit to a biblically faithful church where they will engage in the lifelong process of maturation. It is in the church that spiritual children, who were once "tossed to and fro by the waves", grow to become stable and mature in Christ.

Not only will heaven be directly affected by the church's progress but so will hell. If Jesus' church is God's gift to a sinful world for the maturing and equipping of believers for the work of the ministry, then whenever this fails, hell profits from it. When the church gets side-tracked or distracted and foolishly abandons the gospel for every other wind of doctrine and craftiness of deceitful schemes, hell always profits, glories, and continues to populate.

An eternal place of conscious torment is the reward for every soul who rejects the Good News of Jesus' salvation. Jesus uses the term "*hadēs*" to depict this destructive, ravenous force that opens its mouth wide to consume an untold number of precious souls. It represents the ungodly place of the dead, insatiably devouring the deceived, trapping all who sell out for a counterfeit gospel, and engulfing sinners who reject the forgiveness that Christ offers.

The great news of Jesus' prophecy is that the gates of hell will never ultimately prevail against the church. This does not mean that hell will never overcome local churches and ministers who have abandoned biblical truth for a lie, sin, or the easy path of compromise. In the end, when Jesus returns and receives his kingdom from the Father, the gates of hell will be ultimately defeated. At that time the faithful church will be declared victorious through the blood of the Lamb and the Word of faithful testimony, "for they loved not their lives even unto death" (Revelation 12:11).

The Apostles' Deep Devotion and Passion for the Church

As we consider the speech of Paul in Acts 20, it is not inconsequential that the apostle, who is hurrying to be in Jerusalem, allocated precious time to call the Ephesian elders, to instruct them and offer this final charge. What this shows is that the apostle knew the importance and value of the local Christian church. It was not convenient for him to take this time and to invest it by ministering to these elders, but such was his belief that the church matters—and it matters eternally.

In fact, the Apostle Paul expressed such deep devotion to the Christian church that alongside his many sufferings and persecutions on account of his gospel work, he lists his daily anxiety for the churches:

> ". . . with far greater labors, far more imprisonments, with countless beatings, and often near death. Five times I received at the hands of the Jews the forty lashes less one. Three times I was beaten with rods. Once I was stoned. Three times I was shipwrecked; a night and a day I was adrift at sea; on frequent journeys, in danger from rivers, danger from robbers, danger from my own people, danger from Gentiles, danger in the city, danger in the wilderness, danger at sea, danger from false brothers; in toil and hardship, through many a sleepless night, in hunger and thirst, often without food, in cold and exposure. And, apart from other things, there is the daily pressure on me of my anxiety for all the churches" (2 Corinthians 11:23–28).

For many of us, it might appear quite strange and even ill-fitting that Paul would list alongside his accounts of horrific physical torture the emotional anxiety he feels for the church. If we contrast them side by side, it may show just how inconceivable this is.

- Five times I received at the hands of the Jews the forty lashes less one,
  "... my anxiety for all the churches."

- I was stoned,
  "... my anxiety for all the churches."

- Three times I was shipwrecked; a night and a day I was adrift at sea,
  "... my anxiety for all the churches."

- With countless beatings, and often near death,
  "... my anxiety for all the churches."

There appears to be a stark disparity between suffering the whipping of 39 flesh-tearing, rib-exposing lashes, or shipwreck and bobbing hopelessly in the sea for hour after hour of frightful uncertainty, versus the anxiety for the success and health of the churches. But there was no such disparity in Paul's assessment. He knew full well that the church of the living God is the "... pillar and buttress of the truth" (1 Timothy 3:15b).

Do pastors of modern churches feel this same anxiety for the church of the living God? Do they feel such a profound longing for a purer church, a more biblical church, a more faithful church, a more Godly, more holy, more loving, more fruitful church?

The Holy Spirit within Paul, pressing him on to a life of greater fruitfulness and zealous soul-winning, made any apparent disparity between his physical torments and his anxiety for the church nonexistent. Rather the disparity is really between Paul's anxiety for the church and, in contrast, our less-than fervent regard for it. Don't hurry past this point too quickly. Let this conviction settle on you and bear its full effect. The passion, love, deep concern, and investment of the apostles for the Christian church are unquestionably clear from their example in the New Testament. This is an example that we have been called to live up to and an example we too often exempt ourselves from. Too often we are proffering pathetic excuses to discharge ourselves from this burden. May our repentance be thorough, swift, and permanent.

The Church Is Yet Loved by One Who Is Infinitely Greater Than the Apostles

If we are not adequately stirred by the example of the apostles to cherish, love, and serve the church, then try and consider just how valuable the church is to the God who obtained it at an inconceivably high price.

> "the church of God, which he obtained with his own blood" (Acts 20:28b).

Carefully read these words of the eminent theologian and pastor from 17th century England, Richard Baxter:

> "[Notice] the price that was paid for the Church [of God] which we oversee: 'Which He,' says the apostle, 'obtained with his own blood.' Oh, what an argument is this to quicken the negligent, and to condemn those who will not be quickened to their duty by it! 'Oh,' says one of the ancient [teachers], 'if Christ had but committed to my keeping one spoonful of his blood in a fragile glass, how curiously would I preserve it, and how tender would I be of that glass! If then he has committed to me the purchase of his blood, should I not as carefully look to my charge?' What! sirs, shall we despise the blood of Christ? Shall we think it was shed for them who are not worthy of our utmost care? You may see here; it is not a [minor] fault that negligent pastors are guilty of . . . Every time we look upon our congregations, let us believingly remember that they are the purchase of Christ's blood, and therefore should be regarded by us with the deepest interest and the most tender affection. Oh, think what a confusion it will be

> to a negligent minister, at the last day, to have this blood of the Son of God pleaded against him; and for Christ to say, 'It was the purchase of my blood of which you did make so light, and do you think to be saved by it yourself?' O brethren, seeing Christ will bring his blood to plead with us, let it plead us to our duty, lest it plead us to damnation."[12]

Richard Baxter encourages us to engage in this thought experiment. Take a moment to consider how preciously and tenderly we might care for a small vial of Christ's actual blood. Think, if you will, just what kind of global frenzy would ensue if archeologists could somehow discover and prove beyond any doubt that they had a small vial of Christ's blood. Consider how the whole world would clamor to get their hands on it. Consider how the institutions and governments of man would seek to buy it at any possible price. World religions would claw at each other for a chance to boast of this possession. The Vatican would spare no expense just to complement its collection of superstitious relics. Yet, understand that the infinite Lord and all-wise God considered the church of Jesus Christ of greater worth and value than even this holiest blood. God proved this once for all by willingly spending the blood of Christ to purchase his church.

Will the love that Christ has for his church not elevate our appreciation for it? Will we have the courage to reassess our estimation of the church which, though feeble, broken, and often dis-unified, remains the apple of God's eye? The church, even if it suffers from weakness of leadership, lack of direction from under-motivated overseers, and the rampant sin of its members, remains the tangible result of a transaction God finalized at the cross. There was no meager sum offered for the purchase of Christ's church; it was

12. Baxter, Richard. *Pastoral Ministry: An Anthology from the Reformed Pastor*. Edinburgh: Banner of Truth Trust, 2007. Print pg. 131–132.

nothing short of the holiest blood ever to course through human veins—the sin-free blood of the God-man, Christ Jesus himself.

The church is the purchase of the cross, and as such, no matter how treacherous a state it may be in, let us renew our love and recommit our whole heart and life to serve it and see it prosper.

There is a very popular saying attributed to Charles Spurgeon, with variations in wording to the effect of, "If God has called you to preach, never stoop to be a king." The closest variation that can be tied to Spurgeon might be, "If God has called you to be a missionary, your Father would be grieved for you to shrivel down to be a king."[13] Either way, the sentiment is a worthy one. The Holy Spirit is the Divine Person charged with making overseers. Those who are called into this special, essential, and elevated office must not see their charge as insignificant and they must not think that the churches they serve are inconsequential.

The church of Jesus Christ is God's principal work in the world today, whether the church is great or small, rich or poor, known or obscure. Jesus once comforted his own small band of disciples by encouraging them like this,

> "Fear not, little flock, for it is your Father's good pleasure to give you the kingdom" (Luke 12:32).

Through the ordinary means and ministry of ordinary men commissioned into an extraordinary office, God is bringing about his eternal purposes and advancing his kingdom in this world. Overseers, therefore, must never stoop to do anything else or envy others who occupy what may seem to be the world's loftiest positions.

13. Spurgeon, C. H. *Spurgeon Gold*. United States: Bridge-Logos, 2005. pg. 77.

Overseers, consider what gentleness, kindness, diligence, valiance, and affection your church needs from you. Remember that this church is to God the very thing he spent the costliest sum to procure. Never think trivial thoughts of the church. Never offer hypocritical and heartless service to the church. Always give your best, asking the Lord to continue to grow your love for his church. As this love grows, you will soon discover what Paul meant when he spoke of his enduring anxiety for the churches. You will learn to understand and emulate the depth of wisdom and emotional investment in a phrase like this,

> ". . . my little children, for whom I am again in the anguish of childbirth until Christ is formed in you" (Galatians 4:19).

The Minister's Life

Always on Display

> *"You know, from the first day I set foot in Asia, how I was with you the whole time, serving the Lord with all humility, with tears, and during the trials that came to me through the plots of the Jews"* (Acts 20:18–19).

> *"Remember you are God's sword, His instrument—I trust, a chosen vessel unto Him to bear His name. In great measure, according to the purity and perfection of the instrument, will be the success. It is not great talents God blesses so much as likeness to Jesus. A holy minister is an awful weapon in the hand of God"* (Robert Murray M'Cheyne).[14]

> *"Only let your manner of life be worthy of the gospel of Christ . . ."* (Philippians 1:27a).

The Common Ailment of a Double Life

It is very common for church leaders to think of themselves as having two lives, one public and the other private. Many overseers divide their time and energy between the person they portray in public and retain their true selves for private. This creates superficiality in their service and ministry. This phenomenon is so common that very few take the time to examine whether this is even appropriate, biblical, helpful, or God-honoring.

14. Spurgeon, C. H. *Lectures to My Students: Complete & Unabridged.* Grand Rapids, MI: Ministry Resources Library, Zondervan House, 1954. Print pg. 8.

On the one hand, ministers, like all people, undoubtedly have their right to privacy and should sanctify times of seclusion for refreshment. Overseers must take care of their energy levels, protect their times of rest, and preserve the sanctity of their homes and families. On the other hand, there is a stale professionalism that is becoming prevalent among the ranks of ministers who have dichotomized their entire life between the public ministry they're employed to perform and their private life.

We see no such double life in the example of the Apostle Paul. From day one, and throughout the whole time he lived among the Ephesian elders, Paul's life and conduct were always in full view: "You know, from the first day I set foot in Asia, how I was with you the whole time."

A dangerous myth that many overseers have uncritically accepted is that their flock only needs to engage with them occasionally and superficially. When God summons a person to lay down their life for the cause of Christ, he calls that whole person for the entirety of their life. The Apostle Peter echoes this sentiment in his instruction to elders,

> "So I exhort the elders among you, as a fellow elder and a witness of the sufferings of Christ, as well as a partaker in the glory that is going to be revealed: shepherd the flock of God that is among you, exercising oversight, not under compulsion, but willingly, as God would have you; not for shameful gain, but eagerly; not domineering over those in your charge, but being examples to the flock" (1 Peter 5:1–3).

Ministry is never comparable to the 'day jobs' of the majority of other people. The minister doesn't clock in at the start of the day and then clock out at the end. He is constant, around the clock, on duty for his Lord and serving his people.

To one of his disciples and protégés, Paul encouraged,

> "Show yourself in all respects to be a model of good works, and in your teaching show integrity, dignity, and sound speech that cannot be condemned. . . ." (Titus 2:7–8a).

The important word here is "show." It emphasizes the point that an elder's whole life is to be on display "in all respects." The minister's life is not just on display for spectators to observe, but to be a model of good works.

Paul also stresses that the work of ministry is principally about the integrity and dignity in what ministers preach and teach. Overseers must get the gospel right and proclaim it with all their ability, strength, gifts, and the Spirit's anointing. If overseers cannot get this right, then they have no business being in the ministry at all.

Right doctrine is essential to getting the gospel right. In the overseer's teaching, he must show unblemished integrity and unwavering faithfulness to the Scriptures. This integrity is deeper than just the use of precise words. The minister must teach with both precision and the forthrightness that the gospel warrants. Overseers must ensure that there is dignity to their teaching that elevates it beyond a circus act or a stage performance in a local theatre. A crude portrayal of eternal realities is barely worth more than a comedy routine. God's servants have a perpetual obligation to ensure that their speech has biblical soundness that cannot be condemned or gainsaid. When an overseer is occupying the place of the teacher (which is compulsory evidence of his calling, cf. 2 Timothy 2:24), he must give no undue offense whatsoever in word, posture, gesture, or tone. He must allow the gospel to sound forth in the Spirit's power and make certain that his hearer finds nothing offensive except what is offensive in the gospel itself.

It is unlikely that any overseers would feel a need to counter anything that has been written thus far. There's nothing innately controversial in the claim that gospel ministers, in the public eye, ought to be faithful in gospel proclamation. To Titus, however, Paul also wrote that elders must show themselves in all respects to be a model of good works. This is where Paul's personal life stands in stark contrast with the lives of many serving in church leadership today.

Once overseers have faithfully proclaimed Christ and him crucified, what remains for them to do is to exemplify, by their actions and example, precisely how the gospel is to be lived.

When an overseer considers himself to be little more than a public preacher and office-bearer in the church, he has forsaken the essence of gospel ministry. Conversely, when overseers accept their responsibility to both teach and live out the implication of the gospel, they prove themselves faithful stewards of the calling of the Lord.

The overseer who hides himself away after teaching is a poor example of the triumphant life Christ died and rose to bestow. The minister's life is his sermon's best illustration. By his example, he either ratifies the doctrine he espouses or undermines it. The minister, as a man called by God to shepherd the flock, does not lead well by merely barking orders and detailing instructions to others. Rather, he performs his ministry best by practicing the principles of the gospel and engaging in his own war against Satan, sin, and self in view of his people.

This is not a call for ministers to forsake Sabbath rest and keep their foot hard pressed on the gas until burnout or breakdown renders them useless. Being disciplined to take times and seasons of rest is as much a part of living out the gospel as being frequently engaged in public ministry. When the overseer's people see their leader taking adequate rest to be at his best to continue the mission of Christ, they learn just how crucial disciplined stewardship of our bodies and minds is.

What is even worse than an overseer who will not live his life on display as an example to his flock is the minister whose life is a reproach to the gospel. Ministers who live contrary to the holiness required of Christians will end in ruin whether they think they have successfully hidden it from their people or not. An overseer steeped in sin and shackled in unbelief is a scourge to the flock of God. Ministers who live their lives contrary to the model of good works which Paul exemplified only tear down what they have hoped to build in the ministry of the Word.

A Life Worth Emulating

This raises a vital question: Do we, as overseers, even have lives worth displaying and emulating?

Many overseers are unable to follow Paul's example in this regard because their lives don't amount to anything worth imitating. Every minster should be asking themselves, "If the people I serve were to copy the sum of my life's example, would they be growing in Christlikeness? Would they be getting holier?"

Overseers, let me ask you directly: Are you a holy enough example for your people? Are you a model of the gospel's power in a believer's life to bear good fruit? Are you showing sufficient triumph over secret and slight sins (let alone major habitual sins)? Would you be content for your own life to be entirely put on display for your whole congregation to watch and replicate? If a video camera could be fastened to you so that everything you did, said, and looked at, was live-streamed for everyone to see, would believers be challenged to be more like Jesus by what they saw of your daily life?

We know that the Apostle Paul was able to answer a confident and resounding "yes" to these questions. Therefore, he was able to live those three years amongst the Ephesians with every aspect of his life on full display, encouraging all to imitate him as he imitated Christ.

Some may carp that Jesus is the true and only ultimate exemplar for the Christian life, and our duty as overseers is solely to point to him. There is much truth in this assertion. Jesus is certainly all that, yet this doesn't absolve Christ's servants from looking like Jesus, acting like Jesus, speaking like Jesus, and thus being a conveyance of Christ's practical example to others. In Jesus' day, it was the common practice of disciples to emulate their rabbi with such precision that when a crowd was hearing the disciple teach in place of their master, he should be indistinguishable from the master. Disciples were tasked with knowing not only the teaching content of their master but even his very phrases, words, tone, inflection, pace of speech, and exact gesticulation. In a world without AV recording or artificial amplification, this was how rabbis disseminated their teaching and example far and wide. By training and mobilizing their disciples to be their carbon-copy replicas, rabbis were able to extend the reach of their message and influence exponentially.

The idea of discipleship has undergone a severe downgrade since the times of Jesus. Among today's overseers, there is a grave loss of what it means to emulate Christ for his sheep to see and follow. However, the main issue with the idea that "our duty as ministers is solely to point to Jesus" is that simply was not what Jesus' initial disciples and ministers understood as their calling. Paul explicitly wrote, "Be imitators of me, as I am of Christ," (1 Corinthians 11:1). Every minister, from Paul down through church history ought to be able to encourage the same.

An overseer's life, example, sweat-earned holiness, and teaching are the great deposit into the lives of his people. If ministers fail in one of these areas, they are failing the sheep of Christ and inhibiting their ability to live victoriously over sin.

Elsewhere, Paul stressed to pastor Timothy,

> "Keep a close watch on yourself and on the teaching. Persist in this, for by so doing you will save both yourself and your hearers" (1 Timothy 4:16).

Again, we observe the emphasis that the apostle laid on both faithful teaching and the example of one's practical life. This is the double-edged sword of every minister, which he wields to combat error and lead God's people to the glorious and abundant life Jesus promised (John 10:10).

The assurance that Paul offered Timothy upon compliance with this principle is very striking: ". . . for by so doing you will save both yourself and your hearers."

Are you a faithful shepherd, desiring above all else, the salvation of those you serve? Do you consider it a small matter that some of your flock might descend into the bottomless pit on account of your failure to comply with this clear apostolic command? Can you fathom their bitter accusations against you on the Day of Judgment, as eternal life is irreversibly forfeit, and much blame lies at your feet? Because you chose rather to live and minister as one who gave half his heart, half his time, half his energy, and half his commitment to your calling, you were unable to "save both yourself and your hearers." Are the souls of the people entrusted to your care undeserving of your greatest sacrifice?

Overseers might feel compelled to protest at this line of questioning, assuring themselves that Jesus is the only Savior and that they cannot possibly be held responsible for their people's ultimate destiny. The exclusivity of Jesus as Savior is never in question. However, Paul, under the inspiration of the Holy Spirit, issued this warning to Pastor Timothy for very good reason. There is something unique and powerful in the life of Christ's overseers who pursue holiness and conformity to Jesus in every area of their life. Should they fail to live in accordance with their profession of faith, precious souls will undoubtedly be forfeited from among their flock. There is a certain and mysterious link between the spiritual health, vitality, faithfulness, and fruitfulness of a local church's ministers and the salvation of those in that congregation.

Is it possible for overseers, who claim to be called by Christ and shepherds after his example to have so little of his sacrificial love in them? To save sinners, Jesus died to assuage the infinite wrath of a holy God. Would his earthy representatives dare to live inconsistent with that ultimate sacrifice? Will ministers not strive with all of their energy and faculties to see souls saved?

> "Him [Christ] we proclaim, warning everyone and teaching everyone with all wisdom, that we may present everyone mature in Christ. For this I toil, struggling with all his energy that he powerfully works within me" (Colossians 1:28–29).

Overseers, very soon you, your flock, and the many thousands of unbelievers living within your reach will either be in a place of eternal joy and pleasure or a place of horrific, unending conscious torment.

Overseers must be willing to sacrifice their very life for the salvation of others' souls. They must battle against their own sin, as though the salvation of their flock depended on it. They must be willing to give themselves entirely to their work as Paul himself did when he labored among the Ephesians.

Jesus asked, "For what does it profit a man to gain the whole world and forfeit his soul? For what can a man give in return for his soul?" (Mark 8:36–37).When we consider the reality that a single soul is of more value than an entire world, only a fool would forfeit a soul to gain anything in this world. No pleasure, no prominence, no fame, no fortune, no friend, no family, not even our bodily health or preservation, is worth prioritizing over the salvation of a single soul. If a soul is of greater value than a world of riches, power, pleasure, pomp, and rewards, then how foolish is that minister who exchanges his privilege of laboring to win souls for the petty tokens this earth offers?

Before you protest, remember that Jesus' example embodied this very truth. Jesus willingly sacrificed pleasure, prominence, fame, fortune, and even his bodily health and safety to seek and save you. Recall that as an overseer you are solemnly charged with shepherding the church of God. Therefore, whatever sacrifices you must make for the salvation, growth, maturity, and spiritual prosperity of your people is not only worth it, but it is infinitely less than the sacrifice Christ made. If Jesus can die the horrible death of becoming a curse on the tree to redeem us, then no sacrifice he asks of us is too great.

A confronting example of the necessity for ministers to live lives worthy of emulation is offered in the life of Charles Spurgeon (1834–1892). It is a lengthy anecdote, but well worth quoting in full.

> A young minister had been preaching in a country village, and the sermon took deep effect on the minds of the hearers. In the congregation, there was a young man who felt acutely the truth of the solemn words to which the preacher had given utterance. He sought the preacher after the service and walked home with him. On the road, the minister talked of every subject except the one that had occupied his attention in the pulpit. The poor soul was under great distress, and he asked the minister a question or two, but they were put off very coolly as if the matter was of no great importance Arriving at the house, several friends were gathered together, and the preacher commenced very freely to crack his jokes, to utter his funny expressions, and to set the company in a

roar of laughter. That, perhaps, might not have been so bad, had he not gone even farther, and uttered words which were utterly false, and verged upon the licentious [grave immodesty]. The young man suddenly rose from the table; though he had wept under the sermon and had been under the deepest apparent conviction, he rose up went outside the door, and stamping his foot, said, "Religion is a lie! From this moment I abjure God, I abjure Christ, and if I am damned, I will be damned, but I will lay the charge at that man's door, for he preached just now and made me weep, but now I see what he is! He is a liar, and I will never hear him again." He carried out his threat; and some time afterward, as he lay dying, he sent word to that minister that he wanted to see him. The minister had removed to a distant part but had been brought there by providence, I believe purposely to chasten him for the great sin he had committed. The minister stepped into the room with the Bible in his hand to do as he was accustomed—to read a chapter and pray with the poor man. Turning his eyes on him, the man said "Sir, I remember hearing you preach once." "Blessed be God," said the minister, "I thank God for it," thinking, no doubt, that he was a convert, and rejoicing over him. "Stop," said the man, "I do not know that there is much reason for thanking God, at any rate, on my part. Sir, do you remember preaching from such-and-such a text on such-and-such an evening?" "Yes, I do." "I trembled then, sir, I shook from head to foot; I left intending to bend the knee in prayer and seek God in Christ, but do you remember going to such-and-such a house and what you said there!" "No," said the minister, "I cannot." "Well, then, I can tell you, and mark you! through what you said that night my soul is damned and as true as I am a living man, I will meet you at God's bar and lay it to your charge." The man then shut his eyes and died. I think you can scarcely imagine what must have been the feeling of that preacher as he retired from the bedside. He must carry with him always that horrid, that terrible incubus, that there was a soul in hell who laid his blood to his charge.[15]

15. Haddon Spurgeon, C. *Spurgeon's Sermons Volume 02: 1856.* United Kingdom: Devoted Publishing, 2017. pg. 316.

The Main Thing

Gospel Proclamation

"You know that I did not avoid proclaiming to you anything that was profitable or from teaching you publicly and from house to house. I testified to both Jews and Greeks about repentance toward God and faith in our Lord Jesus" (Acts 20:20–21).

"Preaching is God's great institution for the planting and maturing of spiritual life. When properly executed, its benefits are untold; when wrongly executed, no evil can exceed its damaging results. It is an easy matter to destroy the flock if the shepherd be unwary or the pasture be destroyed, easy to capture the citadel if the watchmen be asleep or the food and water be poisoned. Invested with such gracious prerogatives, exposed to so great evils, involving so many grave responsibilities, it would be a parody on the shrewdness of the devil and a libel on his character and reputation if he did not bring his master influences to adulterate the preacher and the preaching. In face of all this, the exclamatory interrogatory of Paul, 'Who is sufficient for these things?' is never out of order" (E.M. Bounds).[16]

The Primacy of Preaching

It is highly significant that the activity Paul prioritized in building Christ's church was the proclamation of the truth of the gospel. It is also significant what he does not say occupied most of his

16.Bounds, E. M. *The Works of E.M Bounds.* (n.p.): Reformed Church Publications, 2015. pg.5.

time and energy among these Ephesians. For example, there's no mention of programs, schools, flashy methods, community service, gimmickry, attractive entertainment-based techniques, or anything of the sort. Just the straightforward preaching of the gospel—baptized with tears!

This must be noted well. Overseers must abandon the use of everything that distracts and detracts from the holy mandate of fervent, clear gospel articulation. There's nothing inherently wrong with programs, schools, community service, or anything else listed above, but ministers will never know true faithfulness or fruitfulness until they make "*preaching*—baptized *with tears*" their highest priority.

When we speak of preaching, it cannot be reduced to just the 35-minute sermon sandwiched between praise music in a Sunday worship service. This, we trust, is indeed true preaching, but heralding the truth of God's Word is so much more than that. Some ministers are tasked with the weekly exposition of the Scriptures, some are not. But all ministers are called by God to be disseminators and defenders of the truths of the gospel in whatever situation they find themselves. A high view of the power of the preached Word, regardless of the context or setting, is essential to Pauline ministry and fruitfulness. The gospel must be explicitly and compellingly articulated before we can ever presume to be modeling our ministry after the example of the apostles. Explicit and compelling gospel articulation can take place in a wide array of settings and contexts. Only very few will involve a loudspeaker, a pulpit, a well-prepared sermon with three points, and an entertaining story with some edgy jokes. Wherever you find yourself serving as a minister of Christ, never neglect to explicitly articulate the truths of God's Word as life and light to all who have the opportunity to hear.

God's Word is an imperishable seed.[17] God's promise regarding that seed is, "He who goes out weeping, bearing the seed for sowing, shall come home with shouts of joy, bringing his sheaves with him" (Psalm 126:6). This is the Lord Jesus' method for establishing and advancing his kingdom (cf. Matthew 4:17). This is also what the apostles found most profitable for their ministries. In committing their lives to the sowing of the imperishable seed, they bore much fruit in their service as ministers, and this principle remains true today.

Unfortunately, there have been many ministers who look on the ancient practice of heralding the gospel through the primitive use of preaching as old-fashioned and out-of-date. One does not have to go far in searching before they find ministers who presume to have outsmarted God and have created new measures and means for reaching the lost and building Christ's church. The modern church is brimming with examples of ministers who have substituted robust, faithful, Bible-preaching for modern methodologies that diminish the purity of the proclaimed Word and reduce the church to a place of mere amusement. These modern gimmicks are great at drawing a crowd but have no power whatsoever to humble a sinful heart and bring a lost soul into salvation.

If we desire to experience true apostolic power for obtaining apostolic fruitfulness, then we must commit to apostolic methods coupled with apostolic devotion and humility.

The Details of Paul's Preaching Ministry

Initially, it may not seem like the speech in Acts 20 details much about Paul's preaching ministry in Ephesus, yet there is a great deal to learn from the scant details he offers.

17. Luke 8:11, 1 Peter 1:23.

The apostle explicitly mentions 8 things about his preaching ministry in Ephesus:

1. The content
2. The necessity
3. The location
4. The manner
5. The time period
6. The regularity
7. The scope
8. The result

1. The Content

> ". . . repentance toward God and faith in our Lord Jesus" (vs. 21).

Simply put, in his preaching, Paul prioritized the essence of the gospel of Jesus Christ. He called upon his hearers to not hear in vain but to acknowledge their sin by their repentance toward God and obtain forgiveness by faith in the Lord Jesus Christ.

Every sermon, every gospel conversation, and every opportunity for the name of Jesus to be named must be seized as an occasion to proclaim, "*repentance toward God and faith in our Lord Jesus.*" Any sermon that comes short of explicitly making plain the sinners' duty in abandoning self and receiving Christ, is treasonous.

Considered by many to be the Prince of Preachers, Charles Spurgeon had strong words for preachers and ministers who failed to fill their sermons with Christ and his gospel.

> The best sermons are the sermons that are full of Christ. A sermon without Christ is an awful, horrible thing. It is an empty well; it is a cloud without rain; it is a tree twice dead, plucked by the roots.

> It is an abominable thing to give men stones for bread, and scorpions for eggs, and yet they do so who preach not Jesus. A sermon without Christ! As well talk of a loaf of bread without any flour in it. How can it feed the soul? Men die and perish because Christ is not there, and yet his glorious gospel is the easiest thing to preach, and the sweetest thing to preach; there is most variety in it, there is more attractiveness in it than in all the world besides."[18]

There is cause for mourning the great departure from these fundamentals in our own day. The devil achieves his greatest victory over churches and ministers when there is a neglect of the pure principles of preaching, "Christ and him crucified" (cf. 1 Corinthians 2:2). Sadly, what often prevails in the place of Pauline preaching is speculative unending toying with the latest fads, novelties, and fashions.

Ministers who neglect the faithful proclamation of Paul's gospel can never, in good conscience, repeat what he later declared to the Ephesian elders:

> "Therefore I declare to you this day that I am innocent of the blood of all of you, because I did not avoid declaring to you the whole plan of God" (Acts 20:26–27).

The declaration of Jesus Christ as Lord and him crucified for the salvation of sinners was the bedrock of Paul's hope and the core of his message. If he was found preaching any other gospel, or even if an angel from heaven came down and preached another gospel, then the only result is *anathema*—to be cut off from God and relegated to eternal destruction (Galatians 1:8–9).

18. Charles Haddon Spurgeon, "Christ the Glory of His People" *The Metropolitan Tabernacle Pulpit Sermons*. London: Passmore & Alabaster, 1868. pg. 467.

It was Paul's conviction that the Word of God didn't need improvement, modification, modernization, or relativization. It simply needed humble, heartfelt, and zealous proclamation, just as he himself practiced.

For Paul, to preach the simple message of Christ from all of Scripture was preaching the *kingdom* of God. Preaching any other message in the place of the gospel was not only a failure to preach the kingdom of God; it actively establishes the kingdom of darkness.

How does the summary of Paul's preaching, "repentance toward God and faith in our Lord Jesus," encapsulate the entirety of the gospel? These two phrases function as a synecdoche capturing the total essence of saving truth. Although we are told that Paul preached repeatedly, night and day, for three years, we do not have any transcripts of his many sermons. What we do have, as a distillation of them all, are these two clauses,

1. Repentance toward God
2. Faith in our Lord Jesus

Rightly understood, the content of these two clauses covers the full breadth of Paul's gospel preaching. As we mine the depth of these two clauses, we shall discover the rich theology of Paul's sermons preached throughout his time spent with the Ephesian church.

- God

The first clause introduces the incontrovertible truth that the triune God of Scripture lives. Atheism, after all, is the coward's resignation against the light of reason and nature. What is observed in Paul's unswerving proclamation is that the Scriptures offer no toleration for atheistic foolishness.

Just as the Bible itself opens with the declaration, "In the beginning, God . . ." (Genesis 1:1), so the gospel commences its great proclamation on this same foundation. The truth of the existence of an everywhere-present, all-powerful, all-knowing, and eternal being is self-evident. Reason necessitates that there exists an infinite and unchanging Being.

If there were no infinite, all-knowing, and unchanging Being, then reason itself is a myth and nothing remains but sheer irrationality. When created beings, such as humans, process information rationally and function in this world based on immaterial principles (i.e. reason, the uniformity of nature, the law of non-contradiction), they make the fundamental, tacit, and practical admission of God's necessary existence.

The atheist may protest that he has no belief in any god, but his life and actions betray him. He lives as though the immaterial and universal laws of logic exist. He believes nature is uniform and anticipates its consistency. He believes that he himself enjoys real existence and that his existence has meaning and purpose, and he functions accordingly.

The profession of the atheist that there is no God is a profession that is only possible if there is, in fact, a God. For that very statement to be true, truth must exist. Truth must exist beyond the conventions of social constructs. It must exist both eternally and personally. How can truth, which is by nature immaterial, exist anywhere outside of a thinking mind (not a material brain, but an immaterial mind)? Before the creation of the material world, truth existed. Indeed, it had to, for how can transcendental truth come into existence or go out of existence? For truth to exist, it must have existed in an immaterial mind which transcends any material world or chronological boundary.

It is utter foolishness to posit that God, eternal truth, and transcendental meaning do not exist. C.S. Lewis once quipped,

> "If the whole universe has no meaning, we should never have found out that it has no meaning: just as, if there were no light in the universe and therefore no creatures with eyes, we should never know it was dark. Dark would be without meaning."[19]

The Psalmist concurs, saying, "The fool says in his heart, 'There is no God.' They are corrupt, they do abominable deeds; there is none who does good" (Psalm 14:1).

God's existence is the starting point of all knowledge, meaning, and rationality. Therefore, it is at this point that Scripture commences and so does the gospel. This God is not only self-existent, but also sovereign and supreme in his space-less-ness, timelessness, limitless-ness, superlative power, and holiness. That such a God exists is the foundation for all truth and the fear of him is the beginning of knowledge and wisdom (cf. Proverbs 1:7, 9:10).

- Sin

After the acknowledgment of God's existence, the second declaration the gospel makes is that ". . . all have sinned and fall short of the glory of God" (Romans 3:23).

When Paul described the sum of his preaching in the words, "Repentance toward God," what is unmistakably implied in the word "repent" is that some indiscretion has been committed which requires repentance.

19. Lewis, C. S. *The Complete C.S. Lewis Signature Classics*. United Kingdom: HarperCollins, 2007. pg. 41.

The gospel that Jesus and the apostles preached was not a gospel about self-renovation or self-esteem. Sadly, morale-boosting pep talks have become all too common in modern evangelicalism. While they proliferate among many modern churches, they are entirely missing from the pages of Scripture. The message of Christ and his apostles was a forthright denunciation of sin and a declaration of imminent judgment unless Spirit-born repentance performs a thorough work in sinners' lives.

It is in the very nature of true repentance to bring us to the painful realization that, by nature, we are at odds with God and estranged from him. We are sinners through and through. God, who is unassailable in justice and holiness, cannot be passive toward sin and will never allow it to go unpunished. Before the gospel announces its good news, it reveals to sinners their fallenness and total inability to remedy or remove their guilt. The gospel, therefore, is an intervention of the best kind. It arrests us as we career toward damnation by revealing our true nature and our moral bankruptcy before God. It then compels us to look to Christ for the salvation which can never come from within ourselves.

The repentance called for in the gospel is more than just repentance for its own sake. We all have an inner Pharisee that seeks to excel in good works and make a compelling display of outward righteousness. Paul preached that repentance needs to be directed "toward God." If our repentance stems from any other motive than to please God, then we must repent even of our repentance.

An infinitely holy God can't tolerate rebels and sinners indefinitely. He must, at some definite point, put away every guilty one from his presence, for his eyes are too holy to look upon evil (Habakkuk 1:13). A holy God and an unholy person cannot dwell together, and it is foolishness and blasphemous to suggest that God would change his nature to accommodate sinners. It is the sinner, and not God, that must acknowledge fault and seek a comprehensive change. How can a sinner's repentance be considered anything other than sin if the sinner is unable to reform and undo their guilt by their own power? The prophet Isaiah testified, "We have all become like one who is unclean, and all our righteous deeds are like a polluted garment. We all fade like a leaf, and our iniquities, like the wind, take us away" (Isaiah 64:6).

Repentance is a necessity, but how can a sinner repent from a pure motive when even their "righteous deeds are like a polluted garment?" The second phrase provides the answer: ". . . faith in our Lord Jesus."

- Faith

Faith is not a work; it passively receives all that Jesus is and has done for sinners. Paul stated this truth plainly: "For by grace you have been saved through faith. And this is not your own doing; it is the gift of God" (Ephesians 2:8). Faith is the conduit of salvation, sanctifying all our failures and impure motives by crediting us with Christ's perfect righteousness.

Repentance that is born from selfish and sinful motives can never accomplish salvation. In fact, selfish repentance for sin is a corruption worse than the sin itself and will only add to the weight of condemnation on the day of judgment. Repentance that stems from faith, however, is made holy, not by any innate virtue in itself, but by the virtue of the One in whom that faith is exercised.

Faith is the connection between the sinner and God. Through the meritorious life, death, and resurrection of Jesus Christ, faith becomes the hand that reaches out and receives Jesus' righteousness, humility, and merit as its own. The sinner and the Savior become vitally connected through that conduit of faith. Thus, faith receives Christ and his perfect righteousness, and any subsequent actions that it produces are considered righteous by God. The only way our repentance can ever be acceptable to a just and holy God is if it is born from true faith in Jesus, "who became to us wisdom from God, righteousness and sanctification and redemption" (1 Corinthians 1:30). For, "the just shall live by faith" (Habakkuk 2:4).

Consider the necessity of both faith and repentance in sinners drawing near to God enjoying both eternal acceptance by him and fellowship with him. There is no other way for anyone to draw near to God and be found worthy of entrance into God's glorious reward of eternal life.

The necessity of faith is repeatedly affirmed throughout the Scriptures, but one specific reference shall demonstrate it, ". . . without faith it is impossible to please [God], for whoever would draw near to God must believe that he exists and that he rewards those who seek him" (Hebrews 11:6).

Repentance cannot precede faith because the Scriptures are clear that, ". . . whatever does not proceed from faith is sin" (Romans 14:23b). Therefore, repentance must be a result of faith. Otherwise, it is just as sinful as the sin which made it necessary. Once saving faith has been born in the heart of the new convert, their reflex action is to be repulsed by their sin and pursue a life of continual repentance toward God.

This is the promise of God in the gospel which Paul preached and every faithful minister has since reiterated,

> "But to all who did receive [Jesus Christ], who believed in his name, he gave the right to become children of God, who were born, not of blood nor of the will of the flesh nor of the will of man, but of God" (John 1:12).

- The Lord

Jesus, being truly God, came to earth, to bring salvation and freedom (John. 1:1, 11–12). As a human he could suffer and be tempted in every way that humans are, yet being truly God, he was entirely without sin (Hebrews. 4:15). This Lord Jesus was God's solution, and his offer of peace and righteousness to sinners is their only hope of attaining eternal life.

Jesus, although he humbled himself to become the suffering servant, never ceased to be the Lord of all:

> ". . . though he was in the form of God, [he] did not count equality with God a thing to be grasped, but emptied himself, by taking the form of a servant, being born in the likeness of men. And being found in human form, he humbled himself by becoming obedient to the point of death, even death on a cross" (Philippians 2:6–8).

Preaching Christ in a manner consistent with the apostles always entails declaring him as Lord. We must be careful that when we preach or teach about Jesus, we do not mistakenly portray him as a helpless victim or a hapless casualty of God's desire to declare his undying love for sinners. His Lordship can never be in question, whether we are speaking about the eternal Son before the incarnation, the newborn swaddled in Bethlehem, the wandering rabbi and miracle worker in Galilee, or the sacrificial Lamb hanging on the cursed tree. Every moment of the existence of the Son of God, no matter how outwardly weak, weary, or worn he may seem, is a moment of true sovereignty and Lordship. Even at that moment of what appears to be his greatest vulnerability, he wants it on record that,

> "No one takes [my life] from Me, but I lay it down of My own accord. I have authority to lay it down and authority to take it up again. This charge I have received from My Father" (John 10:18).

In his humanity, Christ truly suffered. When we speak of his supreme Lordship, we are not denigrating his authentic humanity. As the unique God-man, who possessed two perfect natures in the one Person, he could fill the role of servant, sufferer, and sacrifice, and yet remain eternally and unassailably Sovereign.

Jesus as Lord is the joyous confession on the lips of all who have been granted saving faith, "for the same Lord, is Lord of all, bestowing his riches on all who call on him. For 'everyone who calls on the name of the Lord will be saved'"(Romans 10:12b–13).

- Jesus Christ

The name "Jesus" means "Jehovah Saves," just as the angel Gabriel instructed Mary, ". . . and you shall call his name Jesus, for he will save his people from their sins" (Matthew 1:21). This Jesus is the prophesied and long-awaited Christ, messiah, anointed one. He came to fulfill the offices of Prophet, Priest, and King. By taking on our human form, yet remaining Lord and truly God, he perfectly fulfilled the law's demands in the stead of sinners, went to the cross to take their punishment and guilt, dying in their place as substitute.

Paul declares this powerfully,

> "And to the one who does not work but believes in him who justifies the ungodly, his faith is counted as righteousness . . . It will be counted to us who believe in him who raised from the dead Jesus our Lord, who was delivered up for our trespasses and raised for our justification" (Romans 4:5, 24).
>
> "Thanks be to God for his inexpressible gift!" (2 Corinthians 9:15).

By these two clauses, "repentance toward God" and "faith in our Lord Jesus Christ," Paul summarizes his entire preaching ministry and captures the essence of the gospel of grace. We know, by his constant witness, and the highest priority he held the gospel in, that Paul prioritized this message every time he had the opportunity to speak about his Lord.

If today's ministers are to be faithful in imitating Paul's example, then they will understand the necessity of being unyielding in their commitment to "know nothing among [our own hearers] except Jesus Christ and him crucified" (1 Corinthians 2:2).

2. The Necessity

We learn from Paul that this gospel *must* be preached at all costs. This he demonstrated by the high risks he took in procuring opportunities to proclaim it. He reminded the Ephesian elders that they could testify that, when it came to preaching the gospel, he "did not avoid" it, or "shrink from" proclaiming it (Acts 20:20, 27).

In these phrases, Paul indicates that he resisted every lesser motive to pursue self-preservation by shrinking back from preaching this gospel (Acts 20:29). The pressure on him was immense, often life-threatening, yet he could not avoid the necessity to preach. "For if I preach the gospel, that gives me no ground for boasting. For necessity is laid upon me. Woe to me if I do not preach the gospel" (1 Corinthians 9:16).

Paul's will had been commandeered by a higher authority and for a greater cause. His life was not his own as he had been purchased at a price. Because of this, Paul openly and repeatedly identified himself as a bondservant of the Lord (Romans 1:1).

Jesus prophesied, "And this gospel of the kingdom will be proclaimed throughout the whole world as a testimony to all nations, and then the end will come" (Matthew 24:14).

This gospel, by the very nature of being the sole message of salvation for sinners, demands to be preached. It is no overstatement to say that eternal life and death hang in the balance. Paul captures this sense of urgency by saying,

> "For 'everyone who calls on the name of the Lord will be saved.' How then will they call on him in whom they have not believed? And how are they to believe in him of whom they have never heard? And how are they to hear without someone preaching?" (Romans 10:13–14).

How could anyone be considered guiltless if, after managing to discover the precious cure for the world's most deadly disease, they kept it to themselves for fear of rejection or mistreatment? How could a person defend themselves from the charge of cowardice and the most inhuman cruelty if they had discovered such a cure but were unwilling to share it with the world because of their timidity?

The parallel to the gospel is as plain as day. Every believer has been called by the Lord to be a proclaimer of this good news as it is the only message by which souls can be saved. Ministers bear this calling to a higher degree. Even so, many indeed shrink back and hesitate in proclaiming the gospel for fear of ill-treatment. Overseers must resolve in their hearts that whatever the personal cost they bear in preaching Christ, it is more than worth it. The expense of life, liberty, and security is of no comparison if by the proclamation of the gospel the Lord is glorified, and souls are rescued from hell. Paul's resolve is clear and exemplary,

> ". . . it is my eager expectation and hope that I will not be at all ashamed, but that with full courage now as always Christ will be honored in my body, whether by life or by death" (Philippians 1:20).

Does the cost to our own personal reputation and material possessions matter in light of eternity? Scripture reveals the resolve of brave Christians who suffered desperately under the tyranny of Nero. They joyfully accepted the plundering of their property because they knew that they had a better possession and an abiding one in glory (Hebrews 10:34). Ministers should acknowledge that we have not always done well at maintaining heavenly-mindedness and have often grown selfish and self-preserving. If through our suffering the gospel reaches more precious souls, how can we hesitate to pay that price (1 Corinthians 9:22)? The promises of Scripture anticipate that this will prove challenging indeed, but they encourage us to preach Christ regardless of the cost, knowing that any "light momentary affliction is preparing for us an eternal weight of glory beyond all comparison" (2 Corinthians 4:17).

Let us emulate Paul's example and never shrink back. Let us sustain the conviction that the gospel is always necessary and always in need of zealous proclamation. Then we shall press forward into the battle becoming ever more "steadfast, immovable, always abounding in the work of the Lord, knowing that in the Lord your labor is not in vain" (1 Corinthians 15:58).

3. The Location

> ". . . publicly and from house to house" (Acts 20:20).

An appreciation for the urgency and necessity of the gospel produces indefatigable zeal. Furthermore, the imperative of 1 Corinthians 15:58 to be "always abounding in the work of the Lord" prevents ministers from being overly preferential about location and setting. Wherever gospel opportunities arise, ministers must seize and redeem them. Tragically, there are many professional "ministers" today who demand to preach only in the fanciest, cushioned, and air-conditioned venues. They demand comfortable luxurious accommodations and require teeming, adulating crowds. This kind of pomp and charade has nothing in common with the life of the Apostle Paul. Paul's philosophy for redeeming every opportunity, regardless of whether it was demeaning or elevating, is embodied in this text,

> "For though I am free from all, I have made myself a servant to all, that I might win more of them . . . I have become all things to all people, that by all means I might save some" (1 Corinthians 9:19, 22).

Furthermore, ministers ought not to expect that their obligations are fulfilled once they've preached their weekly sermons. If location is no hindrance in disseminating the gospel, then overseers must be diligent in zeal to accompany their people into their very homes, and public places, to lovingly instruct them in the Word of God.

Never neglect the power of personal communication of the gospel to one, or a few people, in the privacy of a home. To be sure, there is true power in public preaching, but one must never neglect to believe in the power of gathering small groups in homes to hear and study the gospel of Jesus. Never allow the glamour of public ministry to cause you to disdain the work of private preaching. The Lord uses both means powerfully to convert souls and train Christians.

This was Paul's practice, not only in Ephesus, but everywhere he ministered. He maximized his time and efforts by publicly proclaiming the gospel and then spending time in more intimate settings with smaller groups clarifying and applying gospel truth.

If you choose to neglect one of these avenues for gospel communication, then you are trying to walk on one leg. Let us again commit to imitating Paul as he imitated Jesus.

4. The Manner

> ". . . serving the Lord with all humility and with tears" (Acts 20:19).
>
> ". . . remembering that for three years I did not cease night or day to admonish everyone with tears" (Acts 20:31).

Earlier we recited the promise of God that "he who goes out weeping, bearing the seed for sowing, shall come home with shouts of joy, bringing his sheaves with him" (Psalm 126:6). There's something tremendously compelling and heart-rending when a minister of the gospel is not too proud to be reduced to tears. I do not mean to encourage what is often called "crocodile tears." False displays of emotion have no place in the life and teaching of a minister of Christ. As powerful as sincere emotion can be in moving the hearts of listeners to sympathize with and internalize the truth of what's preached, the outward show of superficial emotion will have a disastrous and callousing effect. Not only does false emotion produce an undesirable result in the hearers, it is also highly, and detestably, dishonest. Those who imagine that their artificial sympathy is undetectable flatter themselves into delusion. An emotion that is forced and disingenuous is a lie requiring swift repentance.

True humility and genuine tears, however, go hand in hand. Genuine tears are those produced by a true perspective of eternity and the reality that every lost soul is rushing toward irreversible condemnation. When we consider that hell is a place filled with unimaginable pain and torments, how can we refrain from joining Paul in his heartbrokenness and tears? Have we any humanity in us at all if we claim to believe in hell and never weep? How can we be so hard of heart to know real people who don't trust Christ and are only a heartbeat away from facing a very real lake of fire, yet remain dry-eyed?

We can imagine the incalculable multitude of souls in hell even right now, all roasting in the flames of judgment without even a second of reprieve, or a drop of water to cool their tongue (Luke 16:23-24). Can we meditate on that most sobering thought and feel no compassion, no heartrending anguish, no pain in our innermost being?

Truthfully, if it weren't for the grace of God, hell is where every one of us would be. Our salvation is not the reward of our righteousness or the wages of our work. We are redeemed entirely by God's free grace. So, we must ask, what causes us to differ from those who are damned? Is it not that someone took the time and pains to communicate to us the love and mercy of God in Christ? Is it not that someone prayed for us, wept over us, desperately pleaded for our soul before God, and made every effort to come and communicate to us the gracious gift given freely in Christ?

Christians the world over would find it hard to object to any claim made so far. Where then are our tears? Where is the anguish of our hearts? Where is our concern? It is no surprise that Paul wept so deeply as he preached Christ's salvation because he believed that message to the core of his being. It is surprising that we, who have equal claim on this gospel, have so few of our own tears to offer. Luke narrates of Jesus, "And when he drew near and saw the city, he wept over it . . ." (Luke 19:41). Shall our own Master put us to such shame? Even as he approached the very city that would bring about his execution, Jesus still found enough compassion to weep.

Ministers, take note of the example of your Lord and his apostle: "He who goes out weeping . . . shall come home with shouts of joy." Do not begin to play-act and generate tears artificially. Instead, pray and seek God that he might give you a deep and thorough burden for lost souls. Ask God to give you a clear view of the inevitable judgment to come, a deeper appreciation for the preciousness of the Gospel, and the severity of your calling.

5. The Time Period

> ". . . from the first day I set foot in Asia" (Acts 20:18).

Paul was never one to hesitate. The day he set foot in Asia was the same day he began to herald the good news to all who would give him an audience.

This is a wonderful example of a man committed to one purpose, never balking when opportunities present themselves. Paul reminded the Ephesian elders about his ministry commencing the moment he set foot in Asia to stir them from inactivity.

How often do we see ministers linger in their preparation work? How often do we see ministers shy away from preaching in preference for all other means of growing the church? How much time and energy is wasted in peripheral activities? Paul's example is crystal clear: ministers should relegate every other priority to the periphery and immediately get busy sounding forth the wonderful news of a Savior who has shed his blood for sinners.

John Piper sent the 'twitter-sphere' into chaos when he published the tweet,

> "As a strategy for missions, Ready, Fire, Aim, is a better strategy than Ready, Aim, Aim, Aim, Aim, Aim, Aim, Aim, Aim, Aim."[20]

As much as Twitter is a wonderful place to be misunderstood and to actively engage in the most superficial debates imaginable, this tweet had the desired effect. John Piper was intending to challenge the status quo of indulgent over-preparation. The gospel is at its

20. https://twitter.com/JohnPiper Tweet posted at 1:01 PM, March 3, 2015, at https://twitter.com/johnpiper/status/572819200261136385

most powerful when it is simply proclaimed in its most primitive form.

Don't wait for an invitation, don't wait for a sign from heaven to act, don't wait for permission—act now! Perhaps you have not been faithful to act on day one, like Paul was, but today is day one of the rest of your life and ministry. Be patient no more. Aim no more. Fire and strike!

Your risen Savior has already commissioned you. As a disciple of the One who possesses all authority in heaven and earth, he has unequivocally declared that you must, "Go therefore and make disciples of all nations . . ." (Matthew 28:18–19a). To this effect, Charles Spurgeon issued a stirring call to ministers,

> "God save us from living in comfort while sinners are sinking into hell! In every minister's life there should be traces of stern labor. Brethren, do something; do something; DO SOMETHING. While Committees waste their time over resolutions, do something. While Societies and Unions are making constitutions, let us win souls. Too often we discuss and discuss, and discuss, while Satan only laughs in his sleeve. It is time we had done [with] planning and sought something to plan. I pray you, be men of action all of you. Get to work and 'act like men'. Old Suwarrow's idea of war is mine: 'Forward and strike! No theory! Attack! Form column! Fix bayonets, and charge right into the very center of the enemy.' Our one aim is to save sinners, and this we are not merely to talk about, but to effect in the power of God."[21]

Some ministers think that preaching the gospel right out of the gate is unhelpful and counterproductive. Paul demonstrated the foolishness of that philosophy. The gospel preached is its own

21. Spurgeon, C. H. *An All-round Ministry: Addresses to Ministers and Students*. Edinburgh: Banner of Truth Trust, 1986. Print pg. 55.

preparation work. The gospel preached does its own tilling of the soil. The gospel preached is the start, middle, and end of the entire work of ministry.

How could we, in good conscience, withhold the Bread of Life from starving souls because we did not believe they were ready to eat? What could possess us to think so highly of ourselves in making such decisions? How many of the souls that are now constrained in the pit of hell were prevented from ever hearing the great news of grace due to false judiciousness by negligent ministers? We are called "messengers" because the sum of our calling is to go and herald this good news. We do not meddle with the message, and we don't withhold it until we suppose our hearers are ready. We are called to give it and give it often, freely, and from the earliest possible opportunity.

6. The Regularity:

> ". . . for three years I did not cease night or day" (Acts 20:31).

Paul did not arrive in Asia to preach the gospel once and then withdraw when he saw he was creating a storm of chaos and persecution. From the first day he arrived in Ephesus right up to his last, he preached unabated and undeterred. There was a holy constancy in the ministry of the Apostle Paul. He preached the gospel of salvation every morning and again every evening. This is a man who was fully convinced that the gospel "is the power of God for salvation to everyone who believes" (Romans 1:16). This is a man who was fully convinced that the same Gospel which some reject in the first instance might still overcome them and bring them to faith in the next instance. Paul's gospel has not lost one bit of its power from his day until ours and, indeed, will remain mighty to save until the Lord returns.

Paul's pattern of behavior here was not isolated or unique to Ephesus. This ministry philosophy of Paul was a pattern that he maintained throughout his entire ministry. When we turn to the end of the book of Acts, we witness Paul in Rome following the very same principles of ministry that the New Testament commends to us all. Paul's ministry in Rome testifies that he has not eased his foot off the gas at all. If anything, what began as a practice of preaching morning *and* evening in Ephesus, had evolved into a practice of preaching from morning *until* evening in Rome (Acts 28:23).

This uptick in activity for Paul no doubt correlates to his being freed from other pressing burdens on his time and energy. In Ephesus, Paul had to work a regular job and supply his own needs through his physical labor. In Rome, Paul was under house arrest and unable to work. In either situation, Paul observed days and seasons of rest, as the finite body and mind need recovery from such arduous labor. Paul's example here is not an invitation to burn out from overexertion. Yet, if we are diligent to rest as the Scriptures command (one day in seven), then ministers will have ample energy to fill the rest of their time in this very labor: striving incessantly to convince sinners to turn to Jesus.

Very few ministers derive the true benefit of rest in their times of repose because they know very little of the labor of feverish activity that ministry demands. The command was for six successive days of work and on the seventh rest. "Six days you shall labor, and do all your work, but the seventh day is a Sabbath to the Lord your God. On it you shall not do any work . . ." (Exodus 20:8–10a).

If the six-day toil that God calls for is not engaged in, then the times and seasons set aside for rest will be ineffectual. Slothfulness is one of the besetting sins of our age. It is a great tragedy that many pastors, ministers, elders, and other church workers cannot be exempt from the charge of laziness.

Certainly, vocational overseers do not have the opportunity to rest on the Lord's Day when God's people gather for worship. They must be active, alert, serving the Lord in his Word and worship. Therefore, they must prioritize a time to rest in the Lord on another day, and they must defend this discipline firmly. Failure to rest will lead to failure in work. Failure to work will lead to failure to rest. Overseers who neglect this rhythm of work and rest do so at their peril and the peril of those they have undertaken to serve.

Paul pursued such regularity in ministry because he was compelled with a passion to reach as many precious souls as possible. In 2 Corinthians 5, Paul gives us insight into his motivations for serving the Lord with the ferocity and determination that he did:

> "Therefore, **knowing the fear of the Lord, we persuade others**. But what we are is known to God, and I hope it is known also to your conscience. We are not commending ourselves to you again but giving you cause to boast about us, so that you may be able to answer those who boast about outward appearance and not about what is in the heart. For if we are beside ourselves, it is for God; if we are in our right mind, it is for you. **For the love of Christ controls us . . .**" (2 Corinthians 5:11–14a, emphasis added).

These two portions in bold open a window into Paul's thinking. He was not ambitious to gain anything from this world. His entire concentration was fixed on the world to come, with special emphasis on two very powerful motivations.

The first motivation was the "fear of the Lord." This speaks to the reality of sin, judgment, and hell. Many today spurn the idea of allowing hell to be a motivating factor in the minister's life, but Paul never suffered from this novel delusion. God is unquestionably fearsome and righteous in all his judgments, declaring that "the soul who sins shall die" (Ezekiel 18:20a). This incontestable truth should shake every sinning person to the core of their being. God is not a judge to be trifled with and he will ensure every sin is fully accounted for. This fearsome God has provided a means for sinners to be freed from their guilt and obtain eternal life. Because God will ensure every sin is fully accounted for, his provision for salvation includes the very death of his son, Jesus Christ, who suffered to take away the sins of all who receive him. Every sin ever committed will be satisfied in God's judgment, either in the sinner personally suffering eternally in hell or in the atoning death of Christ on the cross. Either way, our God is a consuming fire who will ensure his perfect justice is always satisfied (Hebrews 12:29, Romans 3:26).

Every minister must evaluate his calling in the highest possible terms. They must always have an eye to the judgment of God and the fearfulness of his righteousness. Ministers must utilize this powerful truth to spur them on in their ambition to persuade others to be found in Christ and his gracious salvation.

The second motivation driving Paul was "the love of Christ." Our gospel ministry should never be conducted under a depressing cloud of doom and gloom. Hellfire and brimstone should cause all of us to shudder, and we should never be ashamed of their reality. However, this motivator needs to be balanced with the precious, all-alluring love of Christ. God's principal predisposition toward his creation is love, not vengeance or wrath. God's desire is for sinful souls to come to him, through his Son, and receive mercy and grace. The church's overseers are the ambassadors of God tasked with demonstrating and communicating his love to others, urging them to reciprocate, repent, and believe. May this love compel us just as it did Paul to work tirelessly, morning and evening, week in and week out, to bring sinners to the Savior.

7. The Scope

> "I did not cease night or day to admonish everyone" (Acts 20:31).

The scope of Paul's ministry was quite literally "everyone." He didn't allow anyone to be exempt from the necessity of repenting of sin and receiving Jesus Christ. Sin is universal, so the need for its remedy is equally universal. Therefore, Paul made it his life's ambition to preach Christ to all: "Him we proclaim, warning everyone and teaching everyone with all wisdom, that we may present everyone mature in Christ" (Colossians 1:28).

There is a temptation for ministers to focus their energies on their favorite groups of people. They are often seduced into giving a disproportionate amount of their time to those who make them feel the most comfortable and affirmed. This kind of favoritism betrays the universality of the Gospel. Jesus is the Savior for the entire world, of all classes, races, tribes, and peoples. Therefore, the Gospel must travel to them all without distinction or preference.

Paul stressed that he did not favor or prioritize any single group of people. Nor did he shy away from preaching to groups who represented a threat to his safety and well-being. His objective was the salvation of all people, and for this, he strove to abandon any claim for comfort and safety.

The only way any minister can be exempt from blood guilt is if they faithfully proclaim Jesus to all, without fear or favor.

8. The Result

> "Therefore, I testify to you this day that I am innocent of the blood of all" (Acts 20:26).

This is the glorious result that was produced by Paul's ministry. This will always be the glorious result produced by anyone's ministry who adheres to Paul's example. Many overseers have, for one reason or another, been unfaithful in their charge. This unfaithfulness produces guilt and shame that will be the horror of every person stained with it.

At this juncture, we need to reflect on ourselves. We must take some time now to assess our ministry before the Lord. Let us not be satisfied with pithy and pathetic excuses that we know will never satisfy an infinitely holy God. Let us be sincere and severe in our self-examination.

- Have we been faithful to proclaim the whole counsel of God, never omitting hard and unpleasant truths or unpopular passages of Scripture?
- Have we been faithful to declare the exclusivity of Christ's salvation, that none can come to the Father, except through him?
- Have we been faithful to execute our charge with holiness, severity, and genuineness?
- Have we been faithful to conduct our ministry in humility and with brokenness?
- Have we been faithful to be incarnational, living out our lives before our people, rejecting the temptation to offer a cheap portrayal of our professional persona?
- Have we been faithful to proclaim Jesus constantly and explicitly in our gospel articulation?
- Have we striven, above all else, to see Jesus glorified through the salvation of sinners by calling for their repentance toward God and faith in the Lord Jesus Christ?

Those who can answer "yes" to these questions are privileged with sharing confidently in the Apostle Paul's confession, "I am innocent of the blood of all."

Those who cannot answer "yes" to each of these questions but can acknowledge that improvement is needed must go to God in humble repentance, pleading for forgiveness, which they are sure to receive. Then they can reapply themselves and resolve to minister, after the likeness of the spirit and power of the Apostles, dedicated to zealous and faithful ministry. The words of Richard Baxter offer a fitting charge to this end:

> "Up, then, every man that hath a tongue, and is a servant of Christ, and do something of your Master's work. Why hath he given you a tongue, but to speak in his service? And how can you serve him more eminently than in laboring for the salvation of souls? He that will pronounce you blessed at the last day and invite you [in]to 'the kingdom prepared for you,' because you 'fed him, and clothed him, and visited him,' in his poor members, will surely pronounce you blessed for so great a work as bringing souls [in]to his kingdom. He that saith, 'the poor you have always with you,' hath left the ungodly always with you, that you might still have the matter to exercise your charity upon. If you have the heart of a Christian or a man, let it yearn towards your ignorant, ungodly neighbors. Say, as the lepers of Samaria, 'We do not well; this day is a day of good tidings, and we hold our peace.' Hath God had so much mercy on you, and will you have no mercy on your poor neighbors? But as this duty belongs to all Christians, so especially to some, according as God hath called them to it, or qualified them for it to them . . ."[22]

22. Baxter, Richard. *Practical Works of Richard Baxter: Selected Treatises*. Peabody, MS: Hendrickson, 2010. Print pg. 62.

Our Heroic Example

"Only be strong and very courageous . . ." (Joshua 1:7a).

> *"And now I am on my way to Jerusalem, compelled by the Spirit, not knowing what I will encounter there, except that in every town the Holy Spirit warns me that chains and afflictions are waiting for me. But I consider my life of no value to myself; my purpose is to finish my course and the ministry I received from the Lord Jesus, to testify to the gospel of God's grace"* (Acts 20:22–24).

Years earlier, in Jesus' ministry, he set his face like granite to go to Jerusalem (Luke 9:51). Now we see the same is true of his servant Paul. Both Jesus and this apostle were fully aware of what awaited them, and yet neither flinched. This is stunning courage indeed. To an unbeliever, it may look like nothing more than religion-induced suicide. However, this is true courage, the kind which only the Holy Spirit can impart. Furthermore, this is the courage that we all desperately need, whether we realize it or not. Until we attain it, we must relinquish any hope of a revived church and a great ingathering of lost souls.

The great news is that all who seek to follow in the example of the Savior and his apostles are already possessors of the same Spirit. Being indwelt by the same Spirit proves that we already possess a rightful claim to this courage, ". . . for God gave us a spirit not of fear but of power and love and self-control" (2 Timothy 1:7). It is imperative we do not dwell on our fears. Focusing on our fears allows them to fester in our hearts and minds. God commands that his servants be strong and very courageous (Joshua 1:7).

Whichever thoughts or feelings that we allow to dominate us, whether of fear and timidity, or boldness and courage, will eventually take possession of our whole self. Whatever we meditate on the most will bear the greatest fruit in our lives and become the dominant identity we project.

Decide now to meditate on the awe-inspiring example of our Lord and his apostles. Invest your time and energy fixating on the courage-imparting, boldness-infusing example of those who,

> "... through faith conquered kingdoms, enforced justice, obtained promises, stopped the mouths of lions, quenched the power of fire, escaped the edge of the sword, were made strong out of weakness, became mighty in war, put foreign armies to flight. Women received back their dead by resurrection. Some were tortured, refusing to accept release so that they might rise again to a better life. Others suffered mocking and flogging, and even chains and imprisonment. They were stoned, they were sawn in two, and they were killed with the sword. They went about in skins of sheep and goats, destitute, afflicted, mistreated— of whom the world was not worthy—wandering about in deserts and mountains, and dens and caves of the earth. And all these, though commended through their faith, did not receive what was promised, since God had provided something better for us, that apart from us they should not be made perfect" (Hebrews 11:33–40).

What a wonderful heritage the people of God can reflect on to grow in confidence! If we are in Christ, we are also of that ilk. We are of that same Spirit, and thus we are imbued with that same courage.

The lives and exploits of the heroes of faith in Scripture are recorded to fill us with courage. These men and women are not airbrushed or embellished, their sins and failures are on full display. The lesson for all successive generations of believers is not to think of these great examples as naturally exceptional people, but to see what the power of God can do in the life of a weak and helpless sinner.

Elijah's Stirring Example

Consider the example of one such biblical hero, Elijah the Tishbite. His epic showdown with the 450 prophets of Baal on Mount Carmel is a scene almost unparalleled in its display of boldness (1 Kings 18:20–40). Elijah initiated the challenge to them, contesting whose God had the power to answer with fire. The false prophets summoned Baal and received no response. They reduced themselves to utter exhaustion in calling out, lacerating themselves, engaging incessantly in a plethora of recondite, superstitious invocations, all for nothing. Elijah took to mocking Baal, asking the prophets if he'd gone on a journey of some sort, or perhaps was stuck in the restroom (vs. 27). Baal's prophets were fatigued, suffering blood loss, and cripplingly disappointed, and the Scripture records the result of all their devotion, "but there was no voice. No one answered; no one paid attention" (vs. 29).

It was now Elijah's opportunity to show that the Lord alone is God and indeed answers by fire. With Spirit-imparted courage, Elijah set up his altar, saturated it several times with water (in a time of severe drought), and called upon the Lord Almighty,

> "'O Lord, God of Abraham, Isaac, and Israel, let it be known this day that you are God in Israel, and that I am your servant, and that I have done all these things at your word. Answer me, O Lord, answer me, that this people may know that you, O Lord, are God and that you have turned their hearts back.' Then the fire of the Lord fell and consumed the burnt offering and the wood and the stones and the dust, and licked up the water that was in the trench. And when all the people saw it, they fell on their faces and said, 'The Lord, he is God; the Lord, he is God'" (vs. 36–39).

Elijah then turned his attention to the prophets of the false god, Baal. He slaughtered all 450 of them, a feat which would not have been too difficult after these prophets had exhausted and emaciated themselves. He demonstrated unequivocally what faith in the Lord God and courageous obedience can achieve as the nation was revived from its idolatrous stupor.

This Spirit-born courage in Elijah was the same courage possessed by the Apostle Paul. The Spirit imparts this courage to all who are born again and adopted into God's heavenly family: "For you did not receive the spirit of slavery to fall back into fear, but you have received the Spirit of adoption as sons, by whom we cry, 'Abba! Father!'" (Romans 8:15).

You are not Elijah, nor are you the Apostle Paul, but you are the recipient of the same courage they exhibited. Our calling is not to sit idle and wait for this Spirit-born courage to stir within us. We must take decisive action and pursue conformity to Christ by stirring ourselves up by the means of God's truth. The Word assures us that we have not received a spirit of slavery to plummet back into fear, but we have the Spirit of power, love, and self-control (2 Timothy 1:7). By this Spirit, we are empowered to approach God's throne in boldness, knowing confidently that he receives us graciously as his children (Hebrews 4:16).

Once Elijah's earthly work was completed, he was escorted into heaven by a whirlwind and chariots of fire. After he was taken, his protégé, and disciple, Elisha cried out, "Where is the LORD, the God of Elijah?" (2 Kings 2:14). This question divulges Elisha's inner doubts. Elisha had already been promised by his mentor that he would receive a double portion of his anointing.[23] However, Elisha was dissatisfied because once Elijah had been taken away,

23. 2 Kings 2:10.

there was no apparent difference. He seems to have wanted a sign, an experience, or a feeling that would indicate that Elijah's promise was fulfilled. Earlier when the two prophets traveled to the appointed place for Elijah's departure, this mentor divided the River Jordan by the unconventional yet effective means of striking the water with his cloak. Now as Elisha traveled back the way they came, he appeared to be concerned that he had missed out on the promised anointing. When he arrived at the river he also struck at the water and witnessed it divide just as it had for Elijah. It became apparent to all who saw it (particularly the Jericho school of prophets) that the spirit and power of Elijah had very much come to rest on Elisha.

Often, we too struggle with the unbelief of Elisha. We resist stepping out in faith and exercising boldness in our ministrations until we receive some sign or sense that the Lord will meet our boldness with his power. However, God's Spirit is as ever-present today as he was in the days of Elijah. The Spirit is as willing and available to meet faith with power, as he was in the days of Elijah. The promises of God are as true today as they were when he issued them. Every person who is possessed by God's Spirit has the right to the powerful courage and strength that God supplies (1 Peter 4:11). Of course, as ministers today, it is hardly conceivable that our duties are going to lead us to need river-separating power, but the duties we have been called to execute are no less in need of boldness and the Spirit's strength.

As God's dear children, we must exercise this boldness:

> "For though we walk in the flesh, we are not waging war according to the flesh. For the weapons of our warfare are not of the flesh but have divine power to destroy strongholds. We destroy arguments and every lofty opinion raised against the knowledge of God, and take every thought captive to obey Christ" (2 Corinthians 10:3–5).

Is Paul's Level of Courage Exclusive to the Apostles?

Some have tried to excuse themselves from exercising the same boldness and courage that Paul exhibited. They speculate that unless we are apostles, we have no right to apostolic courage.

This kind of thinking is nothing more than unbelief. It is both cowardly and scripturally untenable. The result of such thinking is that it reduces what should be triumphant gospel ministry into that which is pathetic, irresolute, and ineffectual. The truth is that the apostles were not endowed with a unique species of boldness that is peculiar to their apostleship. Their giftings and authority were certainly unique, but the same Holy Spirit that empowered them with great courage does the same for all believers.

There are four reasons why we can be assured that the courage and faith exhibited by the apostles were not exclusive to their unique calling:

1. The apostles were not always exceptionally courageous. If these men who possessed the unique apostolic anointing showed signs of struggle when the occasion called for boldness and strength, then there is no cause for assuming that elevated levels of courage are innate to the apostolic office. To be sure, there were occasions when exceptional courage was shown by these men. But this was not true on every occasion. Thus, we know that they were not living at a perpetual level of supernatural courage, and yet their apostolic office was permanent. We must conclude that the courage they occasionally demonstrated was not necessarily distinct to their office. Peter, the most outspoken apostle, exhibited severe cowardice at his Lord's crucifixion (Luke 22:54–62). Some may protest at the use of this example because it was before the Spirit falling at Pentecost. However, we also see that after Pentecost, Peter was still prone to bouts of gospel-defying timidity. So greatly did Peter indict himself

on one occasion that he even caused Barnabas, another apostle and close friend of Paul, to succumb to his spineless fear:

> "But when Cephas [Peter] came to Antioch, I opposed him to his face, because he stood condemned. For before certain men came from James, he was eating with the Gentiles; but when they came he drew back and separated himself, fearing the circumcision party. And the rest of the Jews acted hypocritically along with him, so that even Barnabas was led astray by their hypocrisy" (Galatians 2:11–13).

Holy Spirit courage, therefore, is not unique to the apostles. Though we do not share their office, we share the Spirit that indwelt them and this was the true source of their courage as well as ours. Just like them we are not guaranteed this courage will be automatic, but it must be exercised by our faith.

2. The second reason we know that the apostles did not enjoy a permanent state of supernatural courage unique to their office is that they appreciated their own lack of courage, leading them to pray for more. This demonstrates that boldness was not innate to their calling. They, like all Christians, had to fervently seek it and exercise it. If boldness wasn't an immediate attribute of the apostolic calling and needed to be summoned through prayer, then we who are not apostles can expect God to answer our prayer for courage as he did theirs: "And now, Lord, look upon their threats and grant to your servants to continue to speak your word with all boldness" (Acts 4:29). What may surprise ministers today is that even the Apostle Paul felt the acute need for greater boldness:

> ". . . praying at all times in the Spirit, with all prayer and supplication. To that end, keep alert with all perseverance, making supplication for all the saints, and also for me, that words may be given to me in opening my mouth boldly to proclaim the mystery

of the gospel, for which I am an ambassador in chains, that I may declare it boldly, as I ought to speak" (Ephesians. 6:18-20).

3. The third way in which we learn that the apostles did not enjoy an otherwise unattainable level of courage is much more subtle. What we see is that the apostles repeatedly wrote to the entire church encouraging them to seek boldness and power from the Spirit by the same means they used: prayer. The apostles were desirous that the rest of the church would be just as fearless and daring as they were. If non-apostolic ministers are instructed to use the same means as the apostles did, and, by going to the same source, then it follows that all ministers should expect the very same result. Paul offered several exhortations to boldness throughout his epistles:

- "Only let your manner of life be worthy of the gospel of Christ, so that whether I come and see you or am absent, I may hear of you that you are standing firm in one spirit, with one mind striving side by side for the faith of the gospel, and not frightened in anything by your opponents. This is a clear sign to them of their destruction, but of your salvation, and that from God" (Philippians 1:27–28).
- "Therefore, my beloved brothers, be steadfast, immovable, always abounding in the work of the Lord, knowing that in the Lord your labor is not in vain" (1 Corinthians 15:58).
- "Be watchful, stand firm in the faith, act like men, be strong." (1 Corinthians16:13).
- "Finally, be strong in the Lord and in the strength of his might" (Ephesians 6:10).

According to these texts, ministers of all ages need to repent of lacking boldness and proffering pathetic excuses bolstered by convoluted theological arguments. The Scriptures are not vague or nebulous. They call for the fiercest, strongest, and firmest levels of courage the Holy Spirit can bestow on a fallen creature.

4. The final reason that we know that apostolic courage is available and bestowed upon all who pursue it is the inspirational example of so many ministers who were not apostles. Such men of Spirit-born power and boldness stir us to believe that the Lord can also use us in history-altering ways. What is often lacking is not accessibility to God-given boldness, but the willingness to believe it is ours in Christ and to exercise it. We could fill volumes with the stories of people like Adoniram and Ann Judson who pioneered the gospel work in Burma, or Hudson Taylor who forged his way into the spiritual darkness of inland China and founded a church that is bearing the fruit of millions of souls to this day. But, we shall content ourselves with just one example for our edification and encouragement: William Farel.

William Farel (1489–1565) was a gospel proclaimer and evangelist. His zealous and uncompromising preaching of the Gospel angered the Roman Catholic priests and monks who desperately wanted to maintain control over the masses through their superstitions. Farel's enemies made several attempts to silence him by assassination. Some of these attempts included poisoning him, mercilessly beating him, and other acts of violence. On one occasion, while he was in the middle of courageously proclaiming the message of salvation in the open air, a would-be assassin approached and aimed a gun at his head. The murderous lunatic, with the nozzle of his gun pointed at Farel's skull, shouted one simple command: that he cease his gospel preaching. Farel refused to even pause his sermon and acknowledge the situation. This enraged the assassin even more. Farel knew the danger he was in, yet he refused to entertain the threats of this man or suspend his preaching in compliance. The gun was fired, and the crowd that gathered was shocked. But Farel remained firmly in his place. By God's providence, rather than a bullet exiting the barrel as everyone expected, the gun exploded and burned the assailant's hand. Farel turned to face his attacker and calmly said, "I am

> not afraid of your shots." Farel's ministry in Swiss Neuchâtel was one of his greatest conquests of the gospel. Though faced with fierce opposition, violence, severe privation, and vehement scorn, the Lord enabled him to firmly root the Gospel there and see countless souls come to saving faith.[24]

What is clear is that one does not need to be inducted into the apostolic office to exhibit the kind of courage and boldness the apostles displayed. The same Spirit dwells in us all and empowers us for service if we would have faith in God's promise to grant this boldness, seek it by prayer, and exercise it when the occasion calls for it.

Courage for What?

If death-defying, world-denying courage is not unique to the apostolic office, then certainly the purpose for which God grants it is not unique to them either.

The courage that the Spirit imparts to every minster is the courage to lay down our lives for the purpose to which Christ has called us, since "he who is called as a free man is Christ's slave. You were bought at a price . . ." (1 Corinthians 7:22b–23a).

This is precisely how Paul described his own life. It was dedicated, as a slave, to the cause and commission of Jesus. The life of every faithful Gospel minister is a hard road, fraught with many difficulties and trials. The one who commences this journey will soon be met with innumerable reasons to divert from it. He will be tempted to be distracted by the world's praise and acceptance. He'll be tempted to take his hand off Christ's plow and turn aside to what seem like other noble objectives. The devil will do everything possible to silence a faithful minister of the gospel, even resorting to imprisonment, torture, and death.

24. Kirchhofer, M. *Life of William Farel: The Swiss Reformer*. United Kingdom: Religious Tract Society, 1837. pg. 08.

Yet, if we fail to maintain a fixed and resolute purpose to testify to the gospel of God's grace, what eternal value does our life have? What ultimate good has been achieved if ministers spend their lives for anything other than what Christ himself came for, suffered for, ascended for, reigns for, and commissions them to achieve?

Anything less than direct, explicit, continuous, and faithful gospel proclamation achieves only temporary results in a world that soon will be nothing more than smoking ash and smoldering cinders. Very soon the end will be upon us. In the Day of the Lord, ". . . the heavens will pass away with a roar, and the heavenly bodies will be burned up and dissolved, and the earth and the works that are done on it will be exposed" (2 Peter 3:10). What will bashful timidity have earned us then? What eternal good will come from the sweeping lack of courage that can be observed in many churches today?

Nothing in this world is eternal except the souls who dwell herein. Therefore, like the Apostle Paul, go and spend and be spent in the service of winning as many as you possibly can. Count any loss, sacrifice, or suffering a glorious privilege for this cause. A life lived any other way is a life of no enduring value, as Paul said to the Ephesian elders,

> "But I consider my life of no value to myself; my purpose is to finish my course and the ministry I received from the Lord Jesus, *to testify to the gospel of God's grace*" (Acts 20:24 emphasis added).

Filling Up What Is Lacking in Christ's Afflictions

Our lives must be a living sacrifice for the cause of Christ's Great Commission. As it was quoted earlier at the end of Chapter 3, Paul described the ethos of his lifestyle by saying,

> "Now I rejoice in my sufferings for your sake, and in my flesh, I am filling up what is lacking in Christ's afflictions for the sake of his

> body, that is, the church, of which I became a minister according to the stewardship from God that was given to me for you, to make the word of God fully known" (Colossians 1:24–25).

To make every possible sacrifice is the high calling of Christ's ministers and the example set down for us by his apostles. ". . . that with full courage now as always Christ will be honored in my body, whether by life or by death" (Philippians 1:20).

It should be restated that the afflictions of Christ are never lacking in any regard to their atoning virtue. When Jesus offered his life as a sacrifice, he successfully paid the full ransom and final payment that sins deserved. This is necessary so that every sinner who comes to Christ and receives the salvation offered by his sacrifice is assured that they are entirely forgiven and set free.

But where Christ's afflictions are lacking is in their sacrificial conveyance of the message of salvation. God has sovereignly decreed that it will be by the sacrificial ministry of his redeemed servants that this great message of salvation will reach the very ends of the earth and redeem people from every tribe, nation, and tongue. That purpose is bestowed upon all who are called to be a minister of Jesus Christ. Do we have the discipline, direction, and devotion to say with this apostle, "this one thing I do, forgetting what is behind and pressing on . . ." (Philippians 3:13b)? Are our lives simply too valuable to ourselves that we hesitate to lay them down for this one eternal cause?

As one preacher so vividly put it, the baton has now been handed down to the ministers of our generation, and it is caked with the blood of the sacrifice of past generations of faithful men and women.

Cowardly self-preservation is the enemy of gospel sacrifice. Gospel results comparable to that of the apostles will only be seen when courageous, selfless, zealous, single-minded devotion is flourishing again amongst God's ministers.

Will our generation be found faithful? The enemy is not conquered by our own blood or sacrifice. Unless we are willing, however, to relinquish our infatuation with this world and its goods and go forth, sacrificially proclaiming the word of our testimony, it will never be said of us that, ". . . they have conquered him by the blood of the Lamb and by the word of their testimony, *for they loved not their lives even unto death*" (Revelation 12:11, emphasis added).

Be on Guard

"Pay careful attention to yourselves and to all the flock, in which the Holy Spirit has made you overseers, to care for the church of God, which he obtained with his own blood. I know that after my departure fierce wolves will come in among you, not sparing the flock; and from among your own selves will arise men speaking twisted things, to draw away the disciples after them. Therefore, be alert, remembering that for three years I did not cease night or day to admonish every one with tears" (Acts 20:28–31).

The riches of [God's] free grace cause me daily to triumph over all the temptations of the wicked one, who is very vigilant, and seeks all occasions to disturb me" (George Whitefield).[25]

Our enemy, the devil, is crafty, indefatigable, and insatiable. The Apostle Peter reminded all Christians to, "Be sober-minded; be watchful. Your adversary the devil prowls around like a roaring lion, seeking someone to devour" (1 Peter 5:8). While the devil is not omnipresent, his designs are ever-present aiming to bring a speedy downfall to Christ's ministers and a collapse of their ministries. Paul understood the ever-present threat that the enemy was to his ministry, resolving to "not be outwitted by Satan; for we are not ignorant of his designs" (2 Corinthians 2:11). He also understood that the same threat looms large over every gospel ministry that is zealous to thwart Satan's aspiration to populate hell.

25. Whitefield, G. *The Works of the Reverend George Whitefield... : Containing All His Sermons and Tracts which Have Been Already Published...* United Kingdom: Edward and Charles Dilly . . . and messrs. Kincaid and Bell, at Edinburgh, 1771. pg. 82.

Our enemy is real, energized, never-slumbering, never-ceasing, ever-scheming, and eager to gain the smallest foothold in the lives of God's ministers.

Being ignorant of Satan's designs is a sure way to be outwitted by him and consequently devoured. Underestimating his passion to instigate the downfall of God's faithful ministers is a certain way to be defenseless and susceptible to the most rudimentary attacks. Satan possesses the trophies of many victories over devout men who started strong and yet ultimately fell prey to the allurements of the world (c.f. Gehazi in 2 Kings 5:20–27 and Demas in 2 Timothy 4:10).

To be "on guard" as the Apostle Paul instructs, we must understand that the gospel-proclaiming church is the devil's foremost target. To reduce its effectiveness and render it obsolete (for the gates of hell cannot ultimately prevail against it, cf. Matthew 16:18), Satan goes after ministers and the church's leadership.

A full-frontal attack against the church is seldom a fruitful strategy. What is often successful is a slow erosion of the holiness and focus of the church's ministers by simple and subtle enticements. This erosion is soon felt and personally experienced by every part of the church's body. Additionally, Satan dispatches fierce wolves among the church who will not spare the flock, creating divisions among the congregation and fostering resentment toward their God-ordained leadership. All of this has a compounding effect on the church's ministers, reducing them to incipient pawns executing Satan's diabolical whims. This is precisely what Paul predicted would happen among the Ephesian elders, "from among your own selves will arise men speaking twisted things."

The Order of the Command Is Vital

The order of Paul's instruction is vital, "Be on guard for yourselves and for all the flock . . ."

By ordering the priorities as Paul does, he is helping the ministers to understand that they are the very first and most important line of defense. This means that they are always the primary target of the enemy. If minsters suffer from cowardice in this conflict or find themselves prone to hesitate when the fighting reaches fever pitch, they must resolve to pray hard, long, and desperately that the Lord will grant them supernatural courage. This war will not be courteous, gentlemanly, or civil. It will not be fought fairly, nor adhere to clearly articulated rules of engagement. The victory will not be easy, but it will certainly be won if God's servants are "on guard" and "pay[ing] careful attention."

This order of priorities is reminiscent of the experience of flying on a commercial airliner. Once the passengers are all seated and the captain has readied the plane for take-off, the flight always commences with a safety demonstration preparing passengers for any emergencies that could eventuate. Every aircraft cabin must be pressurized so that when it begins to reach cruising altitude, the passengers are not dependent on the thinning, less oxygenized air outside. One of the main features of the safety demonstration is a short explanation about the pressurized cabin and what to do in the event of falling cabin pressure. The passengers are informed that oxygen masks will automatically drop down from the ceiling above, and all they need to do is pull the mask firmly toward themselves, strap it on, and breathe normally. Passengers who are traveling with small children or other dependents (perhaps the disabled, infirm, or elderly) are clearly instructed to take care of themselves first before they attempt to offer any assistance to others.

While it is fairly obvious to understand why this is important, parents and caretakers, especially those caring for small children, need this reminder. When protective parental instincts kick in, fueled by the panic of an emergency situation, it will not be easy for them to neglect their children while they get themselves masked up.

Once the oxygen masks drop, the passengers have already begun to suffer mild oxygen depletion and may not immediately realize their danger or become cognizant of it in time. In many cases, long before the urgency of the predicament is apparent, passengers can become dizzy, non-functional, their judgment compromised, or even worse, completely unconscious. If a passenger is traveling with someone who is depending on them for care and they do not first help themselves, they could be rendered useless before they have any chance to provide help to others. This undoubtedly puts their own life, and the lives of their loved ones, at severe risk.

Ministry can be very similar. Thus, Paul issues his instructions to the Ephesian elders in the manner and order that he does. Like passengers on an airplane, overseers in Christ's church must first see to themselves before they offer any care or ministry to others. This may seem counter-intuitive and self-serving, but there is no redemptive or even helpful ministry that can be offered to others that is not first the overflow of a minister's own self-watch and care. One cannot expect to issue clean, healthy water from rusty, contaminated jars. Ministers must see to it that they are living lives of impeccable holiness and devotion before they can be of any service or value to others.

Ministers must take tremendous care that they have not inadvertently given the devil the smallest foothold in their lives (Ephesians 4:27). Remember, even the biggest puppets are controlled by tiny, often invisible strings. If there's an area of a minister's life where he is not on guard against the schemes of the great accuser, then that's precisely the target at which Satan will aim.

Ministers are prone to think of their ministry as occupying only a portion of their time and attention and yet their enemy has established a round-the-clock watch on them, seeking the slightest opportunity to strike. His initial attacks may only seem like small, inconsequential temptations, but any indulgence in them will prove they are the most malignant cancers. It is always the small foxes that ruin the vineyard (Song of Songs 2:15). While we may be vigilant to guard against the predictable and obvious attacks, the little foxes creep in undetected and devastate everything.

The desolation caused by small sins is not only experienced in the life of the minister himself, but also among the flock that he was given charge over. A church without biblically faithful and sin-fighting leadership is rudderless, directionless, incompetent, and ultimately destroyed in due time.

It would be a study in the worst of tragedies to survey the many thousands of formerly gospel-proclaiming, strong, healthy churches that end up in closure each year. It would be insightful to ask those churches and pastors what was the first sin, the first appearance of weakness, the first compromise that was tolerated by leadership that resulted in the slow rot of desolation and final extinction. I wonder if they would even know it. Perhaps the cause was a pastor who couldn't (or wouldn't) curtail his repugnant yet private indulgence in pornography. Possibly it was the elders who took their foot off the pedal in their pursuit of Christlikeness. Maybe it was other leaders who were not corrected promptly when their commitment to church attendance became lax, allowing other priorities to crowd their Sunday schedule. Small, seemingly negligible peccadillos, where drastic action feels unwarranted, often become that single cancerous cell that replicates and reduces the entire church to a corpse.

How often do we sit comfortably in our ignorance, thinking slight thoughts of the power of the enemy to prevail against us? Several times in this book we've been reminded that when the shepherd is stricken, the sheep will always be scattered (Zechariah 13:7). If we remain in ignorance and apathy, we will soon be nothing more than another statistic. Often the greatest tragedy comes when an unbelieving world looks on and develops an unconquerable disgust for churches after seeing what hurt can be caused to an entire community in the wake of a church scandal (Romans 2:24).

For elders to be on guard for the flock of God, they must prioritize being on guard for themselves. They must be vigilant to remember that they are the devil's primary target. They must remain aware that they will be forced to bear the brunt of his war against the gospel-preaching church.

Ministers must, without generating too high a view of themselves or estimating their importance too greatly, follow the example of the Apostle Paul who wrote, "I magnify my ministry" (Romans 11:13b). They must make every effort to be sober-minded, watchful, and diligent to keep themselves free from all sin, defilement, and distraction, giving the devil no opportunity.

Satanic Skepticism

Many Christians, and ministers, in particular, live with a functional denial of Satan and his schemes. Prevailing in the modern church today is the idea that giving any attention to spiritual warfare is primitive, superstitious, and unwarranted in our technologically advanced age. To be certain, there are many Christians and even whole traditions that give far too much emphasis to the Devil, becoming infatuated with him and thus ineffectual in gospel ministry. The common reaction to this overemphasis is to give a passing acknowledgment to the existence of a Devil and then move on to other, less awkward concerns. This overemphasis, and overreaction are entirely at odds with the example and teaching of both Jesus and his apostles. It might be cringe worthy to outsiders when Christian leaders speak openly about the Devil and spiritual warfare, but this cannot be allowed to deter leaders from speaking and acting like Jesus. It is an unacceptable and defeatist posture to adopt when ministers feel embarrassed and skeptical about the reality of spiritual warfare. Moreover, failing to see that even this hesitation is a highly effective scheme of the Devil gives Satan a great victory.

Look closely at what the Apostle Paul wrote to the Thessalonian church: "... we wanted to come to you—I, Paul, again and again—but Satan hindered us" (1 Thessalonians. 2:8). The circumstances surrounding whatever hindered the apostle from making his return visit to the Thessalonians has been speculated and debated time and again. The fact is that Paul simply doesn't say. He doesn't feel the need to. Maybe it was obvious for the Thessalonians and they didn't need reminding. What is clear is that Paul believed, and the Holy Spirit affirmed by inspiring his precise words in the epistle, that the circumstances giving rise to this hindrance were not the ultimate cause of his delay. Satan was. Not only was the Apostle Paul hindered once, but "again and again" the devil thwarted his plans.

Do Christ's ministers today have a category for this? Do they have a sensitivity to this ongoing reality? Do they understand that if this can happen to an apostle, it can certainly happen to them (and certainly is happening to them)? Do they flatter themselves that while Paul was seemingly helpless to gain the ascendancy over Satan in this particular matter, they have never been outwitted, thwarted, outmatched, or hindered by him? Or do they undervalue themselves and their office, supposing that this amount of time and attention given by Satan to the Apostle Paul is never going to be appropriate to expend on them? This is devastatingly sad if true. The gospel heralded by the apostles remains the same today, and it will always be the glorious "power of God unto salvation for all who believe" (Romans 1:16). Satan is not a respecter of persons, he is a shrewd antagonist bent on undermining the gospel's spread, however and by whomever it is disseminated.

If you are a minister in Christ's church and Satan has left you alone, that is nothing less than a stunning indictment against you and your ministry. If Satan has calculated you to be of so little threat, and such little consequence, that he is ignoring you, then you have great cause to repent. Overseers are not called to provoke Satan by an unhealthy fascination with him. They are called to provoke him by their mission to depopulate his kingdom. They do this, not by looking for a demon behind every bush and in every breeze, but by an insatiable zeal, directing sinners to partake of the glory of heaven by the gospel of grace.[26]

Ministers who take this warning to heart will constantly examine themselves and uproot any bitterness, unforgiveness, insecurity, illicit competitiveness, doubt, immorality, and pride. They will submit themselves daily to the searching work of the Holy Spirit through the Word (cf. 2 Corinthians 13:5–6, Psalm 139:23).

If overseers are vigilant to do this, always remaining alert to temptation and sin which is "crouching at the door" (Genesis 4:7), then they will be secure in God's promise to "keep [them] from stumbling and to present [them] blameless before the presence of his glory with great joy" (Jude 1:24).

Paul assured the Ephesian elders of the "savage wolves" who are intent on devouring the flock. Carefully note that he is not advising caution for a potential threat; he is predicting a soon-approaching reality.

It is graphic and confronting imagery when one envisions the picture of Paul's metaphor. Imagine a sheepfold with many defenseless sheep all penned in together, entirely ignorant of any threat.

26. An important caveat is needed here. When we speak of the realm, work, influence, agents, and effect of Satan himself, we use his name as a synecdoche. It might not be that Satan himself is plaguing all Christ's ministers and seeking to hinder their lives and effectiveness. He lacks the omnipresence and omnipotence to accomplish that. But his agents are bent on his cause, and when they do his diabolical bidding it is appropriately called the work of "Satan."

Then savage and ravenous wolves begin creeping stealthily into the fold. These wolves have no other design but to tear the sheep apart and gorge on their flesh. This is the threat facing every church. Paul employed such gruesome imagery because the threat is real, the cause is preventable, and the consequences are eternal.

Church overseers are called to not only be on guard against attacks from outsiders but also from within. Paul warned the Ephesian elders that "from among your own selves will arise men speaking twisted things, to draw away the disciples after them" (Acts 20:30). Jude similarly warned the church, saying,

> "For certain people have crept in unnoticed who long ago were designated for this condemnation, ungodly people, who pervert the grace of our God into sensuality and deny our only Master and Lord, Jesus Christ" (Jude 1:4).

Inside attacks are always more difficult to detect. Ministers must appeal to God for the gift of discernment and an ability to perceive people's intentions and ambitions (1 Corinthians 12:10, 1 John 4:1). Insider attacks will be much more effective at winning the confidence of church leadership and generating favor and prominence among the congregation. Because of this, their attacks have the potential to do much more harm than any external assault.

It is not prudent or practical for ministers in a church to distrust everyone. Some overseers, in the name of maintaining a high alert, live in perpetual suspicion of everyone. The corrective Charles Spurgeon offers here is an important counterbalance: "Avoid with your whole soul that spirit of suspicion which sours some men's lives . . . It would be better to be deceived a hundred times than to live a life of suspicion. It is intolerable."[27]

27. Spurgeon, Charles. *Lectures To My Students, Vol 1–4 (Illustrated)* (Kindle Locations 6621-6622). Kindle Edition.

Living a life of suspicion is non-functional and counterproductive. That is not what the Lord expects of overseers. Rather, ministering with a deep trust in the Lord to grant finely tuned discernment is always more effective. When threats are looming, ministers must be ready to detect them and act swiftly to deal with them. This is precisely what will prevent churches from being divided, swindled, and mercilessly ravaged by demonic assault.

The Weeping Apostle

> "Therefore be on the alert, remembering that night and day for three years I never stopped warning each one of you with tears" (Acts 20:31).

For a moment, can you imagine what it would have been like to serve alongside those Ephesian elders? Can you imagine being an eyewitness to the Apostle Paul, personally standing before you, with the tears of sincerity and desperation running freely down his scarred, deformed, travel-weary face? Imagine him, pleading with you, as though he were begging for his own life, that you would not underestimate how valuable the church is to God. Through his tears and repetition, Paul wants the Ephesian elders to feel the full weight of their duty to protect and labor for the flourishing of this blood-bought church. These two objectives must be every minister's highest priority and concern.

It was no isolated incident for Paul to stand before these elders, bathed in his own tears, striving to impress his warning on them. In Acts 20:31, he is asking them to remember that he *never stopped warning* each one of them, night and day, for three consecutive years.

Do not miss the significance of this. What other single issue so possessed the apostle that he would remind his ministers about it, twice a day, exuding raw emotion? Paul cherished the church so highly, and loved it so deeply, that he gladly poured out his life as a drink offering in its service (cf. Philippians 2:17, 2 Timothy 4:6). He continued this strenuous and constant effort so that these overseers would share in his desperation. He wanted them to "be on the alert", and never underestimate how much the Lord loves his church, or how constantly and lethally the enemy will attack it.

Though we do not have the apostle himself bringing this twice-daily reminder to us, it is no less needful. What we can do is engage in the regular habit of remembering Paul and his tears. We can remember his constant remonstrance against indolence. We can picture him frequently addressing these Ephesian elders and let that image weigh heavily on our hearts. Paul shows that the church is of infinitely higher value to God than we can ever estimate. Every minister ought to be prepared, even at a moment's notice, to lay down their life protecting the flock of God, just as Paul said,

> "Be on guard for yourselves and for all the flock of which the Holy Spirit has appointed you as overseers" (Acts 20:28).

Secure In God

"And now I commend you to God and to the word of his grace, which is able to build you up and to give you the inheritance among all those who are sanctified" (Acts 20:32).

At first glance, this benediction may seem to convey a tone of defeat or resignation. One might sense that after all Paul has said and done, he has nothing left to give and resigns them over to the Word of God's grace. On the contrary, this wise, experienced, and inspired apostle knows very well the power he is entrusting these men to. It was no pithy or glib thing that these men, who will shoulder the potential success or failure of Paul's labors in Ephesus, are commended to God and the word of his grace.

Commended to God

Of course, our entire dependence for everything is always upon God. In him, we live and move and have our being (Acts 17:28). Saying "living," "moving," and "having one's being" in succession is an exhaustive way of stating the obvious; our entire existence is dependent on God. Christians of every era have gladly expressed this. But we must also confess that one harmful side-effect of living in these technologically advanced times is that it tends to desensitize us to any felt dependence on God. It would seem that we have everything we need within our reach, readily available, or, delivered right to our door. We are prone to become intoxicated with the ease with which life's essentials are accessed. This has the propensity of preventing us from sustaining an abiding sense of dependence on God.

Being commended to God, entrusted to him, is the only valid posture and place of safety. It is the manifestation of humility to know that everything good in us and coming from us, is because of God's grace. When ministers serve in their own strength, they inevitably fail and drag others down with them. Every ministerial failure, whether small or great, possesses an inordinate gravitational pull, leaving many desolate and their faith destroyed. A sinful sense of independence remains one of the most tragic results of the original fall of Adam. Since the exile from Eden, humans are predisposed to neglect God in their considerations and overlook their dependence on him. This is a sinful posture of the heart and mind that always corrupts our joy, freedom, and fruitfulness for at least two reasons.

1. It is a lie.

The truth is, we are never actually independent of God in any sense of the word. The very nature of our existence, the fabric of the material world we live in, the air we breathe, and the life we live all verify that we cannot live one nanosecond without God's providential care. This means that every time we neglect to feel and acknowledge dependence on him, we embrace a lie. Living a lie is the most dangerous way to live. Ultimately, living a lie is living at odds with God and his view of reality. Every time we choose to live in deception rather than embrace reality, we feed our delusion and experience malfunction at every level of our existence. The pseudo-world we often create in our imagination falsifies our expectations and renders us powerless to achieve meaningful personal growth. Furthermore, it inhibits our ability to relate healthily to others and our circumstances. It also detaches us from God's point of view of the world, rendering us fruitless and unprofitable in his mission. The corrective is not complicated or hard. Settle it in your mind right now; you are not in control of your life. You are not sovereign. You are not even in control of whether your lungs expand and draw in another breath, whether your heart beats one more time, or whether blood clots, cancerous cells, or any such imminent physical disaster comes upon you. Our helplessness is both real and too easily forgotten. We constantly default to an inflated sense of autonomy. James offers this corrective.

> "Come now, you who say, 'Today or tomorrow we will go into such and such a town and spend a year there and trade and make a profit'— yet you do not know what tomorrow will bring" (James 4:13–14a).

James is not against wise planning and prudent anticipation of future events (this is explicitly encouraged in Scripture, cf. Proverbs 21:5). He is against the sin of presumption arising from a mistaken understanding of who we are in relation to the external world and our stated objectives. The people James is rebuking speak about their lives as though it was owed to them, as though tomorrow is as certain as the current moment. What is missing in all of this is deference to the God who inhabits and rules both now and all of space and time.

> "The heart of man plans his way, but the Lord establishes his steps" (Proverbs 16:9).

When we create and then function out of a false view of reality, we stunt our growth in grace. This false reality we are prone to inhabit implicitly dethrones God by overestimating our sovereignty. Once we begin to function from this point of falsehood, our relationships begin to deteriorate. Suspicion and estrangement will set in when others do not endorse our false reality. Those who affirm our self-deception become little more than enablers of our addiction to autonomy. People will often assent because they crave a relationship of reciprocity, resulting in two addicts nurturing each other's destructive dependency. Failing to acknowledge God's exhaustive sovereignty over all things inevitably warps our interpretation of reality. Worst of all, this pride is treason against

God and works directly against his purposes for our lives and ministries. After all, "all such boasting is evil," even when boasting is not explicit or verbalized (James 4:16).

If our harmful and self-indulgent pseudo-independence disconnects us from reality, how should we correct this so we function well in life and ministry? How do we acquire God's view of ourselves and live in that reality? James proceeds to offer clarity on God's view of our life and remedy our perpetual delusion.

> "What is your life? For you are a mist that appears for a little time and then vanishes. Instead, you ought to say, 'If the Lord wills, we will live and do this or that.' As it is, you boast in your arrogance. All such boasting is evil. So whoever knows the right thing to do and fails to do it, for him it is sin" (James 4:14b–17).

That swiftly evaporating vapor that is produced when a kettle is boiled; that short-lived puff of gas that appears when a match is struck against the box; that is the sum of our earthly life. A dissipating mist and a vanishing vapor. This should not discourage us, because that mist which is our lives can be of infinite utility and value in the hands of God. God is intent on our lives bringing him glory and bearing eternal fruit, regardless of how vanishing and futile they might otherwise be. The foremost way in which we achieve these two objectives is by aligning our time, talents, treasure, and energies with the same purpose for which Christ came. While an abundance of speculations are debated as to the main purpose of God's Son entering our world, it was Jesus' own opinion that "the Son of Man came to seek and to save the lost" (Luke 19:10, cf. John 3:17). Put simply, Jesus desired that the chief outcome of his life was to bring maximal glory to his Father by ransoming and redeeming an unimaginable number of precious souls.[28]

28. John 17:5, Revelation 7:9–10, Hebrews 10:5–10.

Any ministry that makes Jesus' Great Commission its central and all-prevailing objective garners fruit for eternity. This life, in contrast to eternity, is smaller than a quark.[29] But this life can be a seed you sow to see the salvation of precious souls. Every one of these invaluable souls will spend eternity giving glory to God. There is nothing else in comparison that's worth living for. For this mission to be successful in your life, your dependence must be entirely on God. Here's the rub: in your own strength, you cannot alter the state of the heart of the simplest child. Without the Spirit empowering your ministry to bear the fruit of saved souls, you are helpless. Yet, without this missional focus, the vapor of your life will evaporate into oblivion and, although you may be saved, you will have little of eternal value to show for your life. Dependence on God's sufficiency and providential care is everything. To live in denial by exalting your own autonomy is to live the false reality of self-sufficiency and always produce the fruit of destruction, never the harvest of righteousness.

> "The fruit of the righteous is a tree of life, and he who wins souls is wise" (Proverbs 11:18, NKJV).

Not only does failing to sustain a due and reverential appreciation for God's sovereignty cause our lives to be filled with deceit, malfunction, and fruitlessness, but also:

2. It deprives ministers of the benefit and positive experience of ministry.

Confronting the reality of the vaporousness of our lives is not to discourage anyone. Nor should it cause ministers to resign themselves to the indolence of nihilism. The realization that God is maximally sovereign over all things and that he has joyously

29. Quarks are the smallest discoverable particles in the universe. They are considerably smaller than the protons and neutrons in which they are found.

called us into his service yields deep and abiding comfort. This understanding is intended to give you a clearer view of reality. This clearer view will help you function as God has purposed: to bring him glory, to bring yourself greater joy and peace, and to bear lasting fruit for his kingdom.

Our joy and satisfaction in God must never be derived from how valuable we think we are to him. Our joy and satisfaction in God comes from how good and gracious he is to us. There is great benefit in the humbling apprehension that God could continue advancing his kingdom, just as he planned and foreordained, with or without us. Apart from the God-man, Jesus, no human being will ever be indispensable to God's purposes. Yet, shockingly, God's eternal plan and foreordination does indeed include you. He has chosen you, not out of any necessity, but out of the sheer abundant pleasure of his heart to see you useful in his cause.

> "By this my Father is glorified, that you bear much fruit and so prove to be my disciples" (John 15:8).

Commended to God for Our Sufficiency

As we have learned, it is God's good and abundant pleasure to call weak, unworthy vessels like us. If we feel adequate to serve Jesus and his cause in our own strength, we show ourselves to be puffed up with pride. Any sufficiency in ourselves that gives us confidence is incredibly dangerous and must be mortified by the Spirit (Romans 8:13). The internal war that rages between our flesh and God's Spirit is a war for autonomy. The flesh boasts and depends on its own perceived sufficiency. When Paul commended the Ephesian elders to God, he was implicitly calling them to remain vigilant in this war.

Jesus makes it painfully clear what worth, benefit, and fruitfulness is achieved outside of him,

> "I am the vine; you are the branches. Whoever abides in me and I in him, he it is that bears much fruit, for apart from me you can do nothing" (John 15:5).

There is perfect freedom, empowerment, and undeterred confidence in knowing that one's sufficiency is never sourced from within, but entirely from God. Paul explains to the Corinthian church where his own sufficiency and confidence came from,

> "Such is the confidence that we have through Christ toward God. Not that we are sufficient in ourselves to claim anything as coming from us, but our sufficiency is from God, who has made us sufficient to be ministers of a new covenant, not of the letter but of the Spirit. For the letter kills, but the Spirit gives life" (2 Corinthians 3:4–6).

This confidence that the apostles enjoyed was unaffected by the world because it was never sourced from there. We have these great and precious promises of not only full satisfaction in God (when we make God the primary source of our satisfaction), but also the grace needed to fulfill our calling to bear much fruit.

As ministers of the church of God, more so than in any other calling, we must actively and frequently remind ourselves that we are God's servants, in God's house, doing his will, and surrendering all we are to his unimpeachable sovereignty. There is no place in the ministry of Christ for self-sovereignty and self-sufficiency. Many ministers allow pride to fester and grow its deadly gangrene in their lives because they have not adequately comprehended, as Paul did, "I know that nothing good dwells in me, that is, in my flesh . . ." (Romans 7:18). Whatever good dwells in us is God's gift of grace, and we deserve no special applause, no special commendation, no glory whatsoever. Like Jesus, the total sum of our joy and sustenance is exclusively in doing the Father's will (John 4:34, 5:19).

The need for humility is at the forefront of all that Paul has communicated to the Ephesian elders. He stressed earlier in his speech that humility was the mark of his ministry among them ("serving the Lord with all humility" vs. 19). If ministers of Christ's church today fail in this elementary point, they fail in everything.

The downfall of King Herod offers a compelling illustration of how vehemently God hates and is utterly intolerant of pride.

> "About that time Herod the king laid violent hands on some who belonged to the church. He killed James the brother of John with the sword, and when he saw that it pleased the Jews, he proceeded to arrest Peter also. This was during the days of Unleavened Bread. And when he had seized him, he put him in prison, delivering him over to four squads of soldiers to guard him, intending after the Passover to bring him out to the people. So Peter was kept in prison, but earnest prayer for him was made to God by the church . . . Now Herod was angry with the people of Tyre and Sidon, and they came to him with one accord, and having persuaded Blastus, the king's chamberlain, they asked for peace, because their country depended on the king's country for food. On an appointed day Herod put on his royal robes, took his seat upon the throne, and delivered an oration to them. And the people were shouting, 'The voice of a god, and not of a man!' Immediately an angel of the Lord struck him down, because he did not give God the glory, and he was eaten by worms and breathed his last" (Acts 12:1–5, 20–23).

Note first the vicious antagonism Herod showed to the Lord's people. The Lord does not take it lightly when his children are persecuted, a sentiment with which any good father can identify. Elsewhere Paul discloses God's ruthless attitude toward those who persecute his people:

> "God considers it just to repay with affliction those who afflict you . . ." (1 Thessalonians 1:6).

> "Beloved, never avenge yourselves, but leave it to the wrath of God, for it is written, 'Vengeance is mine, I will repay, says the Lord'" (Romans 12:19).

When Herod took it upon himself to afflict God's children, he incensed God in a way that no mortal could fathom. In seeking to harm God's anointed church, Herod was storing up wrath for the day of wrath. Notice, however, what brings this King's actual downfall. It wasn't killing the Apostle James, or imprisoning the Apostle Peter with the intent to kill. It was becoming a glory-thief. There is little doubt that Herod's days were already numbered as a sinner who had tempted God to fierce wrath, but his death warrant was sealed only once he seized God's glory for himself. The Lord wasted no time dispatching this king as the text tells us, "Immediately an angel of the Lord struck him down."

We must learn our lesson from the gruesome end of Herod. There is no doubt he felt sovereign, protected, powerful, and secure; yet after one instance of appropriating and savoring the glory that belonged to God alone, he was done. While serving in the ministry, we may be elevated, flattered, praised, honored, and subsequently tempted to let pride flourish in our hearts. Again, we must consistently remind ourselves that whatever good the Lord does in and through us is entirely his work, and all the glory and praise must be passed on to him. If we are faithful in our ministerial duties, people will undoubtedly come to us and offer their appreciation. They may even feel obliged to single us out for exceptional praise. This at times cannot be avoided and can be a healthy show of gratitude, but we must inwardly seek to be nothing more than conduits directing all glory to God. Thus, in reminding the elders at Ephesus of their dependence on God in all things, Paul resolutely commits them to God.

Commended to the ". . . Word of His Grace"

Once commended to God, what is the principal means God uses to humble, teach, secure, empower, embolden, direct, and equip his ministers? His Word. By the working of his Word in our hearts, lives, and ministries, God achieves his purposes and plans for building us up, establishing the church, and advancing his Kingdom. According to Paul, the Word of God's grace produces two distinct results in the lives of ministers who are surrendered to it.

- It builds us up.

The Word of God's grace builds and establishes his ministers into faithful and fruitful servants. It strengthens our faith and compels toward Christlikeness. The Word points us to Christ by providing an ever-increasing understanding of who Christ is. This enables our obedience to him and sharpens his image in us. For the Word to work through us, it must first do its work in us.

Our approach to the Scripture must be consistent with everything we profess to believe about it. If the Scripture is God's very Word, communicated to us and calling us to believe and obey, then our duty and delight are to apply it to every aspect of life. Very few Christians would fail to reverence and be overawed if an earthly king summoned them to hear his personal edict regarding them. Yet, we are prone to forget that the Scripture is the Word of an infinite King, the ruler of all things seen and unseen. Our homage to the Scripture must therefore be as unhindered and reverent as our homage to God. God's Word must not be seen as merely an obligation on us, but as our very sustenance and life. Like food is to the body, the Word of God's grace (the Scriptures) is the source of nourishment to our souls. In appreciation for what value and power the Scripture has, Paul commanded Christians to "let the Word of Christ dwell in you richly . . ." (Colossians 3:16).

There's an increasingly popular, yet ineffectual, way in which God's people relate to the Word. There is a passive way in which believers read over the words, lines, and pages of Scripture seeking only trivial and transient benefit from them. The Scripture must be employed in such a way that it penetrates our very being and bears fruit in every area of our lives. The attitude with which you approach the Bible will go a long way to dictating what value and benefit it is for you.

Paul's promise to the Ephesian elders is that the Word of God can build them up in substance and steadfastness. Inferior substitutes, methods, and philosophies will always fail. God's infallible Word can never lose any of its potency. What it was able to do for the Ephesian elders it is still able to do today. It will sustain and edify all who use it rightly. When all other motivations to persist in the hard slog of ministry fail, the Word will always be able to build you up. It can comfort us when disappointment and depression set in. It can energize us when we feel like there's no longer any point in keeping our hand to the plow and pressing onward.[30] It can keep us from the sin that ensnares and entangles us, and it will set us back on the straight and narrow.[31]

The psalmist asked,

> "How can a young man keep his way pure? By guarding it according to your word. With my whole heart I seek you; let me not wander from your commandments! I have stored up your word in my heart, that I might not sin against you. Blessed are you, O LORD; teach me your statutes!" (Psalm 119:9–12).

Where ministers lack purity of heart and find themselves enslaved to sin, great or small, one thing is sure: they have neglected the

30. Luke 9:62.
31. Hebrews 12:1.

discipline of guarding their hearts according to God's Word. They have failed to store up God's Word in their heart.

Never underestimate the strength of the Word of God. Minister, you need your Bible more than any other book and more than any other source of encouragement and comfort. More than any other place of refuge and respite, the Bible must be your first and last recourse for grace. It must always be near you, always open, ever residing in your heart and life. God's Word alone can build you up into an indomitable fortress that sin and Satan will never overcome.

- It gives us an inheritance.

God's Word not only works in and through us to bring about the obedience of faith; it also works to produce an indescribably glorious inheritance in the world to come. God's Word is more than information. It is God personally acting in us, by his Spirit, "both to will and to work for his good pleasure" (Philippians 2:13).

When a father offers words of comfort to his frightened child, or words of chastisement to a wayward child, these words are offered to provoke and produce an expected outcome. The father desires to achieve the very thing that his words describe. Although they are deeply meaningful to their children, all earthly fathers' words remain finite. Only God's words are infinite and eternal.[32] When God speaks light into creation, the only possible result is that light will manifest. When God speaks the material world into existence, that world instantaneously emerges as the direct result of God's command. When God speaks life into soul-dead, sinning rebels, just like Ezekiel's dry bones, they live.[33] Earthly fathers strive to have their words perform their heart's desire in

32. Matthew 24:35, 1 Peter 1:23.
33. Ezekiel 37.

their children; in contrast, God's Word always performs that for which he intends it.[34]

The promise Paul offered the Ephesian elders is that the Word of God resident in them is producing a special inheritance. Generally speaking, all believers are included in the words, "the sanctified." Paul makes constant use of the doctrine of the believer's eternal inheritance as a means of encouragement.[35] What he is now promising the Ephesian elders is that those who serve as leaders and ministers in the church are set to inherit a unique and special inheritance. This inheritance, produced by the Word dwelling powerfully in them, will be distinct from "*among* all those who are sanctified."

Something very similar is echoed in Peter's first epistle. He singles out local church elders for special commendation and exhortation, saying,

> "So I exhort the elders among you, as a fellow elder and a witness of the sufferings of Christ, as well as a partaker in the glory that is going to be revealed: shepherd the flock of God that is among you, exercising oversight, not under compulsion, but willingly, as God would have you; not for shameful gain, but eagerly; not domineering over those in your charge, but being examples to the flock. And when the chief Shepherd appears, you will receive the unfading crown of glory" (1 Peter 5:1–4).

Unpacking Peter's entire passage is beyond the scope of this book, but the reference to an "unfading crown of glory" that the chief Shepherd reserves and dispenses to elders is particularly compelling. The elders who rule well are those who have submitted

34. Isaiah 55:11.
35. 1 Corinthians 6:9–10; 15:50; Galatians 3:18, 29; 4:30; 5:21; Ephesians 1:14, 18; 5:5; Colossians 3:24; Titus 3:7.

themselves to God's Word in its entirety. They do not seek glory for themselves; rather, their prevailing desire is that the kingdom of Christ would advance through their ministry. Paul instructs Timothy, "Let the elders who rule well be considered worthy of double honor, especially those who labor in preaching and teaching" (1 Timothy 5:17). When Christ appears, he shall bring with him a special crown, a special reward, a unique inheritance for all ministers who have laid their lives on the altar of sacrifice for Christ's cause and kingdom.

This inheritance, which human language could never justly portray, will so overwhelm ministers that, upon receiving it, they'll be so thrilled that they invested their lives to obtain it. The New Testament, in a variety of ways, encourages ministers to consider their eternal reward as motivation to be diligent in their duties. Dangling this rich and heavenly reward before the eyes of the church's ministers is no empty gesture. It is offered to spur them on and assure them that when the day arrives for them to be "crowned," they'll deem all their labor, pains, trials, and troubles a very trivial price to pay.

God's Word is the most dependable thing he has granted us, not only because it sustains the material world we live in (thus it's more dependable than the fixed laws of nature), but also because it establishes the very promises of a God who cannot lie, err, or change.[36] Stand firm then on God's Word, depending on it entirely without the slightest hint of doubt. You'll never be stronger, more unconquerable, steadfast, immovable, or fruitful than when the Word of God is your delight (1 Corinthians 15:58, Psalm 1:2).

For overseers, the road is long, the fight is fierce, and the task is almost entirely thankless. The discipline and zeal required are more than one can naturally muster. Only Scripture can sustain

36. Hebrews 1:3, Numbers 23:19, Malachi 3:6.

us in our calling. The Word of God is the power we need to protect against ravenous wolves and repulsive errors. It is inexhaustibly "profitable for teaching, for reproof, for correction, and for training in righteousness, that the man of God may be complete, equipped for every good work" (2 Timothy 3:16b–7).

Only the Word of God will sustain us so at the end of our race we can say with the Apostle Paul,

> "I have fought the good fight, I have finished the race, I have kept the faith. Henceforth there is laid up for me the crown of righteousness, which the Lord, the righteous judge, will award to me on that day, and not only to me but also to all who have loved his appearing" (2 Timothy 4:7–8).

Prayer

"After he said this, he knelt down and prayed with all of them" (Acts 20:36).

The apostle's instructions are clearly laid out and all his grave warnings are issued, but the real work is only now just beginning. Paul had not fully benefited these elders until he had escorted them by prayer, to the throne of grace. In prayer, he submits them to the Lord who keeps them and gives them the power to abide by all they've been instructed (Jude 1:24).

It is, in one sense, remarkable how highly Paul prioritized prayer. If there ever lived a man who might be tempted to depend on his natural giftedness and acuity, surely Paul would be that one. He possessed a colossal intellect, was thoroughly educated, had tenacious zeal, and was unrelenting in his convictions. This was all true of him even before he was converted and filled with the Holy Spirit (cf. Acts 22:3). Paul, however, knew better than to lean on his gifts; he was a man who made prayer his deep and abiding pleasure.

E.M Bounds explains,

> "The chief of the Apostles needed prayer. He needed the prayers of others, for this he practically admitted in asking for their prayers. His call to the apostleship did not lift him above this need. He realized and acknowledged his dependence on prayer. He craved and prized the prayers of all good people. He was not ashamed

> to solicit prayers for himself nor to urge the brethren everywhere to pray for him."[37]

Are we of this same heart and mind? Doesn't Paul's example rebuke our own prayerlessness? How often does prayer sink low on our list of priorities? How often do we seek success and triumph through our own ability? How often do we neglect the one thing most needed (Luke 10:42)? We would all do very well to recall that our Lord said, "apart from me you can do nothing," (John 15:5). How frequently do we find ourselves neglecting prayer and set our hearts and hands to labor without due consideration of what will make those efforts fruitful?

Horatius Bonar, prolific soul-winner in 19th century Scotland wrote,

> "Nearness to [God], intimacy with him, assimilation to his character—these are the elements of a ministry of power. . . . Our power in drawing men to Christ springs chiefly from the fullness of our personal joy in him, and the nearness of our personal communion with him"[38]

Communion with God is the principal thing. Communion with God through prayer is never to be relegated to the periphery of our responsibilities. Even after all our pontificating on the power of the Word of God in the previous chapter (for which we make no retraction), there is the risk that God's Word might become nothing more than a dead letter if the Spirit does not enflame and enliven it.

37. Bounds, E. M. *The Works of E.M. Bounds*. (n.p.): Reformed Church Publications, 2015. pg. 129.
38. Bonar, H. *Words to Winners of Souls*. United States: P&R Pub, 1995. pg.12.

It is important to recall that the ministry of the Word of God is not automatically profitable. The Jewish authorities of Jesus' day were condemned by our Lord because,

> "You search the Scriptures because you think that in them you have eternal life; and it is they that bear witness about me, yet you refuse to come to me that you may have life" (John 5:39–40).

The Word of God, absent the Spirit's power, profits no one. The power of the Word of God is resident in the Person who breathed it and enlivens it to perform his will (2 Timothy 3:16).

If our ministries are prayerless, we have no reason to expect that God will empower any of our services. If the Lord chooses to use a prayerless minister, it is despite that person, and all eternity will bear witness to that.

As we stressed earlier, every minister needs to maintain a child-like dependence on God, and this dependence is demonstrated through prayer. Without prayer, all our teaching is mere talking, all our instructing is idle, all our warnings profit nothing. Yet when everything we do is bolstered by prayer, we "are more than conquerors through him who loved us" (Romans 8:37).

A minister's love for his people is most clearly demonstrated by how fervently and frequently he labors for them in prayer. Everything else we do for them cannot be considered profitable until we have commenced and crowned our efforts with prayer.

Is there any surprise to see Paul punctuate his most solemn and weighty speech with a word of prayer? This is the same apostle who charged the Christians of Colossae to, "devote yourselves to prayer; stay alert in it with thanksgiving" (Colossians 4:2).

Our duty, following Paul's example, is not merely to pray *for* the people we shepherd, but also to lead them *in* prayer. It is not enough to simply spend our time in private prayer for people. We must also pray with them and alongside them. Paul didn't board the ship that day and assure the elders of Ephesus that they can count on his private prayers for them. He did vastly more. He knelt down, ushering them to follow him, and poured out his heart for them, even while they listened and shared in that sacred moment.

The truth is, if we fail in this one exceedingly important duty, we have failed as ministers of the Gospel. If we teach our people that every other duty in the Christian life is more important than prayer, and they begin to live by this example, we have been treacherous to them and have led them down a path of spiritual bankruptcy. Therefore, we must pray for them in secret, and often in their presence.

We should be willing to expend a great amount of time and energy in prayer. Our duty is not exhausted once prayers are prayed for our people. We should also fervently pray for the many around us who are still unsaved. Should these precious souls not also have a prominent place in our pleadings with God? We have already conceded that we are not powerful enough to convert a single soul without God's help. Salvation is a miracle. The new creation is as much a work of God as the original creation (2 Corinthians 5:17). We need God's power, which is accessed through importunate prayer, to do the work of fruitful ministers.

"Try [Prayerful] Tears"

William Booth (1829–1912), the formidable evangelist and founder of the Salvation Army established "rescue missions" all over England. These missions had one primary objective: to rescue sinners from destitution and destruction by proclaiming the Gospel and offering tangible charity. On one occasion, he had sent out a couple of officers to establish a brand-new work. In their new field, these officers were met with fierce opposition and stiff failure. Frustrated and tired, and seeing no possibility of success, the officers wrote to General Booth requesting that he close their rescue mission and reassign them. General Booth sent back a telegram containing two simple words, "TRY TEARS". The two officers were doubtful at first, but they obeyed their leader and sought God with fresh vigor and zeal. They held nothing back, and through their prayer, seasoned with tears over the lost state of the teeming masses around them, God answered, and sent a mighty revival.[39]

Ministers, are you familiar with seasons of deep anguish over the hopeless state of unforgiven sinners on the brink of spending an eternity in indescribable torment? Have you truly reckoned with the realities of hell? Have you taken time to consider the deep and irreversible consequences of sin, as well as the unfathomable conclusion to life lived without the forgiveness only Jesus offers?

Jesus knew well the condemnation of the wicked because they would not come to him as the exclusive means of salvation. This reality reduced him to anguish and tears. "And when he [Jesus] drew near and saw the city, he wept over it" (Luke 19:41–48).

Here is the harsh and inflexible truth: the vast majority of people in the world right now, each with an immortal soul, are on the fast track to condemnation. Anyone who has spent an honest moment meditating on this and acknowledges this to be scriptural truth has been reduced to tears of anguish and sorrow. These emotions are not an end in themselves. They must give rise to deep, heart-rending prayer to God for his sovereign intervention.

Paul didn't shy away from this truth or the burden it lays upon ministers of Christ. He wrote: "For many, of whom I have often told

39. Story told by H. Begbie in "The Life of General William Booth" as recorded at http://www.jesus-is-savior.com/Great%20Men%20of%20God/general_william_booth.htm.

you and now tell you even with tears, walk as enemies of the cross of Christ" (Philippians 3:18, c.f. 2. Corinthians 2:4). Can the church's ministers today be dry-eyed in the face of such a confronting truth?

How many in your church's neighborhood, in your city, in your state, in your nation, and the nations of the world walk as enemies of the cross? Do they not get a single tear from you? In the words of Leonard Ravenhill,

> "Could a mariner sit idle if he heard the drowning cry?
>
> Could a doctor sit in comfort and just let his patients die?
>
> Could a fireman sit idle, let men burn and give no hand?
>
> Can you sit at ease in Zion with the world around you damned?" [40]

Remember that the Scriptures unequivocally state that the Lord takes no pleasure in the death of the wicked. God's pleasure is that they would turn from their wickedness and live (Ezekiel 33:11). God achieves this through the prayers, sacrifice, and faithful ministries of his servants. Will you pray for them? Will you pray with deep anguish and tears? Are the never-dying souls, that are without hope and outside of Jesus, worthy of your compassion? Maybe you often feel helpless to persuade and compel so many lost people to come to Jesus. Maybe you feel like you do not have the power to make them believe (which, indeed you do not), but there is One who does: almighty GOD. He beckons us to come to him and plead our case on behalf of sinners. Spurgeon gives guidance on this matter, saying,

> "If we cannot prevail with men for God, we will, at least, endeavor to prevail with God for men. We cannot save them, or even persuade them to be saved, but we can at least bewail their madness

40. Ravenhill, L. *Why Revival Tarries*. United States: Baker Publishing Group, 2004. Pg. 92.

> and entreat the interference of the Lord. Like Jeremiah, we can make it our resolve, 'If ye will not hear it, my soul shall weep in secret places for your pride, and mine eye shall weep sore and run down with tears.' To such pathetic appeals the Lord's heart can never be indifferent; in due time the weeping intercessor will become the rejoicing winner of souls. There is a distinct connection between importunate agonizing and true success, even as between the travail and the birth, the sowing in tears and the reaping in joy. 'How is it that your seed comes up so soon?' said one gardener to another. 'Because I steep it,' was the reply."[41]

The history of the biblical narrative is replete with stirring examples of people who approached God in fervent, heartfelt, tearful prayer and were granted their request. Hannah wept, and even in the deep distress of her prayer, she was mistaken as one who has consumed too much alcohol.

> "In her deep anguish Hannah prayed to the Lord, weeping bitterly."

> "As she kept on praying to the Lord, Eli observed her mouth. Hannah was praying in her heart, and her lips were moving but her voice was not heard. Eli thought she was drunk and said to her, 'How long are you going to stay drunk? Put away your wine'" (1 Samuel 1:10, 12–14).

Mordecai wept, and subsequently saw the rescue of his people through Esther,

> "When Mordecai learned of all that had been done, he tore his clothes, put on sackcloth and ashes, and went out into the city, wailing loudly and bitterly" (Esther 4:1).

41. Spurgeon, Charles. *Charles Spurgeon: Lectures To My Students, Vol 1–4* (Illustrated) (Kindle Locations 959–960). Kindle Edition.

Ezra wept, and God granted the repentance and salvation of the entire city of Jerusalem who had spent a generation—including the priests—in sin and harlotry,

> "While Ezra was praying and confessing, weeping and throwing himself down before the house of God, a large crowd of Israelites—men, women and children—gathered around him. They too wept bitterly" (Ezra 10:1).

Jesus wept, not only as he was overlooking Jerusalem, but also throughout his entire ministry. The author of the epistle to the Hebrews justly summarized Jesus' life as one full of fervent cries and tears,

> "During the days of Jesus' life on earth, he offered up prayers and petitions with fervent cries and tears . . ." (Hebrews 5:7).

George Whitefield, one of the most fruitful evangelists ever to preach in the English language, knew how to weep for souls. At times right in the middle of his preaching, for which tens of thousands of souls had gathered in the open air, he would throw his head back and weep uncontrollably for their souls and exclaim,

> "How can I help weeping when you will not weep for yourselves, though your immortal souls are on the verge of destruction!"[42]

And God granted him a harvest of countless precious souls, snatched from destruction.

Who Is Worthy of Your Tears?

For whom shall you weep? What is a sufficiently deep-felt cause that will reduce you to tears? Will you weep for . . .

42.Bridges, C. *The Christian Ministry: With an Inquiry Into the Causes of Its Inefficiency*. United States: Jonathan Leavitt, 1831. pg. 117

- Yourselves? Will you weep for your sins and your lack of concern for lost souls? Are you bothered by your lack of feeling toward the lost? Is this a cause worth your weeping and repenting of? Often a pious weeping over the lost starts when we shed tears over our own cold and calloused hearts.
- Your loved ones? Do you consider your family and closest friends worthy of your tears and fervent cries to God? How many of your family and friends have faith and would be secure in Christ if they met with death today? Have you wept over those who are in imminent danger of hell? Have you carried their names to God and begged him for a powerful gospel intervention so that you will not be eternally separated when you are sent to your respective eternal destinations?
- Your neighbors? Think right now of those living closest to you. Do they trust in Christ? If not, can you imagine seeing their faces aflame in the horrible intensity of hellfire? Should they go to hell without you laboring with all your tearful might to see them converted to God? Should they not be the recipients of special blessing, for no other reason than that they are your neighbor, and you are eager to be obedient to love them and serve them? What kind of neighbor are you to them if you will not even pray that God arrests them in his grace?
- Your countrymen? Paul confessed that his own countrymen, his fellow Jews, held such a deep place of affection in his heart that he would happily surrender his own salvation if it would confer repentance on them (Romans 9:1-3). Can we say the same? Do we have a burning zeal to see our nation come to faith and obtain Christ's blood-bought salvation? Can we pray in deep and sincere anguish for those who share our national identity? God has decreed that we would be co-citizens with our countrymen. Do we not consider it our duty to pray to God to convert our nation hoping that they will all soon be co-citizens of Christ's kingdom?

- Strangers? What about people whom we have never met? Though we do not know them, are they condemned to miss out on the benefit of our prayers? Do we not have a single tear to shed for these precious souls? Are we cold and indifferent toward them because we do not know them? Is it because they do not speak like us, act like us, think like us, or interact with us that we don't care if they are plunged into a pit of ultimate horror? May our tears flow for them, and may they flow often. Let us be constant before the throne of grace and beg God to intervene, that heaven might be populated with myriads and myriads of souls, each as a branch plucked from the fire (Zechariah 3:2).
- The world! And what about our entire world sunk low in sin and destined for destruction? Jesus instructed his followers to pray, "Your kingdom come, your will be done on earth as it is in heaven" (Matthew 6:10). While Jesus has global intentions for his grace, we believers often have a very localized and siloed view of God's kingdom. We fail to understand God's desire is that all the kingdoms of the world will become the kingdom of Christ (Revelation 11:15). Do we have a God who is powerful enough, loving enough, and merciful enough to perform a sweeping and saving work in this world? If so, what has hindered us from going to the Lord, honoring his omnibenevolence and omnipotence, and pleading with him to bring his kingdom here and now? Do the repeated prophesies of a world full of God's glory not stir us to believe and pray for an awakening that covers the earth as exhaustively as water does the sea (Habakkuk 2:14)? How often have we neglected to pray that God would grant this awakening that sweeps in unnumbered masses of souls from every tribe, nation, and tongue (Revelation 5:9)? Do we not believe that Jesus is to have the total pre-eminence in all things (Colossians 1:18)? Do we not believe that total pre-eminence must also include, in the final analysis, the redeemed outnumbering the condemned?

> Do we imagine that Jesus' redemption will yield less fruit than the devil is able to deceive into hell?[43] If we can believe that God loves the world and that the greatest revival God has ever bestowed upon his church is yet to come, then we can obey Jesus' command to pray that his kingdom would come and increasingly encroach upon all the kingdoms of the world. Let us pray compelling prayers in brokenness to a God who desires that the wicked would turn and become recipients of gospel grace. Let us pray that he would bring a sweeping revival (Ezekiel 33:11).

Prevailing prayer is travailing prayer. Paul described his grief over the Galatian Christians who were straying from the truth. They were loosening their grip on the gospel, so he prayed over them that God would intervene and restore them to the narrow way of grace. We referenced this verse earlier, this time pay careful attention to the way Paul describes his anguish in prayer as a woman in the labor pains of childbirth. Paul wrote, "my little children, for whom I am again in the anguish of childbirth until Christ is formed in you" (Galatians 4:19).

43. The prevailing presumption of most Christians today is that hell will undoubtedly outpopulate heaven. Although at a popular level this view remains almost entirely unchallenged, many of the best theologians of Christian history have believed that for Jesus to have pre-eminence in all things (Colossians 1:18), his worshipping throng in heaven, at the end of the age, must outnumber the condemned in hell. To quote a longer portion from a Spurgeon sermon, one sees how fervently he rejected the popular notion of our own day.

> "I confess, I have no wish for a very small heaven, and love to read in the Scriptures that there are many mansions in my Father's house. How often do I hear people say, 'Ah! straight is the gate and narrow is the way, and few there be that find it. There will be very few in heaven; there will be more lost.' My friend, I differ from you. Do you think that Christ will let the devil beat him? That he will let the devil have more in hell than there will be in heaven? No; it is impossible. For then Satan would laugh at Christ. There will be more in heaven than there are among the lost. God says, that 'there will be a number that no man can number who will be saved;' but he never says, that there will be a number that no man can number that will be lost. There will be a host beyond all count who will get into heaven (*The Lost Sermons of C. H. Spurgeon Volume V.* United States: B&H Publishing Group, 2021).

Can we identify with such anguish and heartfelt prayer? Do we have this soul-sorrow over backsliders and the unconverted? If we will not weep for the lost, then let us weep for ourselves that God would give us a heart like his, a heart that loves the sinful world.

The Essential Ingredients of Prevailing Prayer

Thomas Watson, the godly Puritan author and pastor, wrote that the kind of ". . . prayer [that] is most likely to prevail with God [is one] which is rightly qualified."[44] Watson identified seven key ingredients that prevailing prayer must contain to be rightly qualified.[45] Space fails us to delve deeply into all seven, but we will focus our attention on the two that are most pertinent to the discussion of "effectual, fervent prayer" (James 5:16 KJV).

44. The Thomas Watson Collection. Illustrated: *The Ten Commandments, A Divine Cordial, The Godly Man's Picture, The Lord's Prayer and other works.* (n.p.): Strelbytskyy Multimedia Publishing, 2021.

45. The seven ingredients are:

1. Faith (expectancy)
2. Melting (see above)
3. Zeal (see above)
4. Sincere (the one praying must genuinely desire, at a heart level, to obtain the thing prayed for and must not presume God will grant the petition if it is simply based on a whim)
5. Fixedness of mind (the one praying must not be double-minded and must be as determined as the one in Jesus' parable who woke his neighbor pleading for bread and refusing to be denied Luke 11:5–8)
6. Argumentative (the one praying must be prepared to plead with God and make a strong case for the thing requested. He must not presume that simply because it is his desire, God should grant it, but he must be prepared to go to God, ready to demonstrate the thing requested will bring God glory, extend his Kingdom, and he must show his request has due warrant from the Scriptures)
7. Reformation (his prayer must be premised upon his own repentance and asking for forgiveness. The obstinate and unrepentant person will never achieve anything with God through prayer. If we have unconfessed sin, unrepentant sin, let us make this our priority when we approach God even before we seek from him anything else)

Watson wrote that prevailing prayer must contain both attributes of "melting" and "zeal" in the heart of the one praying. He elaborated on what he meant by "melting," explaining,

> "[Prevailing prayer] must be a melting prayer. The sacrifices of God are a broken spirit (Psalm 51: 17). The incense was to be beaten to typify the breaking of the heart in prayer. Oh! says a Christian, I cannot pray with such gifts and elocution as others; as Moses said, 'I am not eloquent;' but can't thou weep? Does thy heart melt in prayer? Weeping prayer prevails. Tears drop as pearls from the eye. Jacob wept and made supplication; and had power over the angel" (Hosea 12:4).

Regarding "zeal" as another essential attribute of prevailing prayer, Watson further expounded,

> "Prayer must be fired with zeal and fervency. 'Effectual fervent prayer avails much.' (James 5: 16) . . . Prayer without fervency, is like a sacrifice without a fire. Prayer is called 'a pouring out of the soul,' to signify vehemence (1 Samuel 1: 15). Formality starves prayer. Prayer is compared to incense, 'Let my prayer be set forth as incense' (Psalm 141: 2). Hot coals were to be put to the incense, to make it odoriferous and fragrant; so, the fervency of affection is like coals to the incense; it makes prayer ascend as a sweet perfume. 'Christ prayed with strong cries' (Hebrews 5: 7). 'Such a cry pierces the clouds' (Martin Luther). Fervent prayer, like a [explosion] engine set against heaven's gates, makes them fly open. To cause holy fervor and ardor of soul in prayer, consider,—Prayer without fervency is no prayer; it is speaking, not praying. Lifeless prayer is no more prayer than the picture of a man is a man. One may say as Pharaoh, 'I have dreamed a dream' (Genesis 41: 15). It is dreaming, not praying. Life and fervency baptize a duty and give it a name."

Never Tolerate False Emotion

We addressed this previously, but it bears repeating here as well. It is never affectation that God is seeking, but genuine affection. God is never honored by the fleshly manufacturing of tears. Displays of emotion that have no sincerity behind them are a lie and a mockery to God. More than that, substituting authentic emotion for a superficial performance is a brutal scorning of the lost who are in desperate need of our sincere affection and prayers.

There are billions of immortal souls inhabiting our planet today. Each one of them is worth more than the value of the entire world itself (Mark 8:36). Each soul will stand before God and give an account for their life (2 Corinthians 5:10). Those who do not have their sins forgiven will be resigned to an inescapable and unrelenting hell. If this doesn't fill your heart with anguish-provoking travail, and at times, even deep wailing, I do not know what will.

There is no place for false and artificial emotion in the life of Christians who confess to believe in the irrevocability of God's eternal judgment. Furthermore, Christians claim to believe in the utter depravity of the unregenerate human heart. They confess to believing in the exclusivity of Christ's salvation and the absolute need for sinners to repent and trust in him. What place can inauthentic tears and affectation have for Christians who have so much to be burdened by?

Go to your knees, ministers, and pray with a forceful emotion that storms heaven for grace and yields a harvest of souls.

Conclusion

How Did the Ephesian Elders Fare?

The church of Ephesus was one of the most fortunate of all the New Testament churches. The Apostle Paul himself founded it, laboring incessantly among them for three years. Additionally, it received more encouragement, direction, leadership, and assistance than almost any other church in the first century. In fact, no other church has ever received as much Scripture personally addressing them and the people in their church. They received their own epistle titled, "The Letter to the Ephesians." Then, they received two more epistles from Paul to his protégé Timothy (1st and 2nd Timothy). Many scholars believe that the intended destination of the Apostle John's three New Testament epistles was also the church of Ephesus. And, of course, one final epistle directly from the Lord Jesus himself to the Ephesians in the book of Revelation. This final epistle, appearing at the end of the apostolic age gives us insight into how well those elders, who stood, listened, and prayed with Paul at Miletus, fared. Depending on whether one embraces the earlier or later dating of the Book of Revelation, this final epistle might represent a review of the church's health somewhere between 15–35 years after the events of Acts 20.

Let us see, then, how Jesus described the state of the church,

> "To the angel of the church in Ephesus write: 'The words of him who holds the seven stars in his right hand, who walks among the seven golden lampstands.

> 'I know your works, your toil and your patient endurance, and how you cannot bear with those who are evil, but have tested those who call themselves apostles and are not, and found them to be false. I know you are enduring patiently and bearing up for my name's sake, and you have not grown weary. But I have this against you, that you have abandoned the love you had at first. Remember therefore from where you have fallen; repent, and do the works you did at first. If not, I will come to you and remove your lampstand from its place, unless you repent. Yet this you have: you hate the works of the Nicolaitans, which I also hate. He who has an ear, let him hear what the Spirit says to the churches. To the one who conquers I will grant to eat of the tree of life, which is in the paradise of God'" (Revelation 2:1–7).

At best, the diagnosis is a mixture of good and bad. They are credited for their plodding perseverance and discernment against false apostles and antipathy against the vile Nicolaitans.[46]

However, the thrust of Jesus' indictment against the Ephesian church is that they have, ". . . abandoned the love [they] had at first". This is no small charge in Jesus's assessment. The Lord treats this so seriously that he warns that if they do not repent, he "will come . . . and remove [their] lampstand from its place". This warning Jesus conveyed is the threat that he will remove their church from before his presence. Every single church that is faithful to God's Word, submitted to Christ's Lordship, is represented before the throne in heaven in the form of a lampstand (Revelation 1:12). Jesus calls every one of these churches to be obedient, faithful, pure, and fruitful.

46. Although they were quite the prominent scourge in the later years of the apostolic era, very little knowledge of the doctrines and practices of the Nicolaitans has survived from antiquity. What we can assume from the scant evidence available is that they were sexually perverse, hungry for sordid gain, and compromised in the face of Roman persecution.

The church in Ephesus had a very strong start, perhaps as strong as any other church ever existing. In both spiritual power and the proliferation of Christ's gospel, the Ephesian church was a true standout. Some years later, by the time of the writing of the book of Revelation, it was beginning to waver, not in doctrine but in fervency and affection. It had begun to falter in its love for Christ and each other.

Thus, this final epistle to the church of Ephesus represented Jesus issuing the church one last chance. We can say with certainty, and with deep sadness, that there no longer exists an Ephesian church today.

What Went Wrong?

Did they neglect to keep watch over themselves and soon lapse into a lukewarm, lethargic state? Did they neglect the love they ought to have for the truth, for the lost, and the church? Did they begin doing church-ish things and cease to function as the true church of Christ? Did they enter the detestable, demon-inspired competitiveness that so many pastors and ministers are prone to today? Did they fail to preach the whole counsel of God, fixating on those passages that lend themselves to popularity rather than confronting sin and dealing with the harder issues?

Whatever it was, we cannot know for certain, but we do know the story ends in tragedy. Every church that is founded on faithfulness and submitted to the Lordship of Christ must be faithful until the return of Christ. Churches that show remarkable health, vitality, and perseverance have God's grace to endure through successive generations of challenges, strife, and external pressure. Somewhere along the line, the Ephesian church (though almost certainly not with the same elders that were addressed in Acts 20) failed to continue growing, pursuing holiness, and seeking to glorify their Savior. They failed to persevere in the purity of doctrine and life, provoking Christ to finally remove their lamp stand. Between the time of Paul's meeting with the Ephesian elders in Miletus, in Acts 20, until the recording and delivery of the Book of Revelation, major cracks were starting to appear. The final consequence of the church was judgment, which always precedes God's final judgment which is coming upon the world.

> "For it is time for judgment to begin at the household of God; and if it begins with us, what will be the outcome for those who do not obey the gospel of God?" (1 Peter 4:17).

Will this be the unfortunate end of the churches and ministries we currently serve? Do we believe that Jesus has the power and full intent to punish churches in our day the very same way he has done throughout history? How solemnly should we take heed of this warning and learn from the example of the Ephesians? This church, among all the New Testament churches, was highly favored and blessed, having every chance to grow, remain stable, and press on until the Day of the Lord, yet they fell short.

The final consequence that the Ephesian church suffered makes for a gripping sequel to the lessons that the Apostle Paul sought to teach the elders that day in Miletus. We would all do well to learn, not only the lessons Paul explicitly shared with the elders of Ephesus but also the hard lessons regarding the dissolution of this church as well. If we do not heed it well, we and our ministries shall all likewise fail.

I leave you then, with this solemn warning and charge:

> "Pay careful attention to yourselves and to all the flock, in which the Holy Spirit has made you overseers, to care for the church of God, which he obtained with his own blood" (Acts 20:28).

And,

> "... now I commend you to God and to the word of his grace, which is able to build you up and to give you the inheritance among all those who are sanctified" (Acts 20:32).

Additional Resources Page

Recommended Further Reading:

- "The Reformed Pastor." Richard Baxter
- "Words to Winners of Souls." Horatius Bonar
- "A Word to Fellow Pastors and Other Christian Leaders." Horatius Bonar
- "The Soul Winner." C.H. Spurgeon
- "Lectures to my Students." C.H. Spurgeon
- "An All Round Ministry." C.H. Spurgeon
- "The Greatest Fight in the World." C.H. Spurgeon
- "Simplicity in Preaching." J.C. Ryle
- "The Divine Art of Preaching." A.T. Pierson

Lightning Source UK Ltd.
Milton Keynes UK
UKHW020805230123
415815UK00016B/609

9 781632 965516